# SELF-DELIVERANCE
## *made simple*

DESTINY IMAGE BOOKS BY
# DENNIS AND DR. JEN CLARK

*Releasing the Divine Healer Within*

*The Supernatural Power of Peace*

*Deep Relief Now: Free, Healed, and Whole*

*Live Free*

# SELF-DELIVERANCE
*made simple*

*Keys to Closing Every Door to*
THE ENEMY IN YOUR LIFE

DENNIS & DR. JEN CLARK

DESTINY IMAGE® PUBLISHERS, INC.

P.O. Box 310, Shippensburg, PA 17257-0310

*"Promoting Inspired Lives."*

*It's Supernatural* and Messianic Vision Inc.

4301 Westinghouse Blvd.

Charlotte, NC 28273

This book and all other Destiny Image and Destiny Image Fiction books are available at Christian bookstores and distributors worldwide.

Cover design by Eileen Rockwell

Interior design by Terry Clifton

For more information on foreign distributors, call 717-532-3040.

Reach us on the Internet: www.destinyimage.com.

ISBN 13 TP: 978-0-7684-1128-7

ISBN 13 eBook: 978-0-7684-1129-4

For Worldwide Distribution, Printed in the U.S.A.

1 2 3 4 5 6 7 8 / 21 20 19 18 17 16

# CONTENTS

# PREFACE

The Protestant Reformation began to restore the truth of the priesthood of the believer. In practice, however, most believers are an audience instead of an army. The times are changing. *Deliverance Made Simple* is not intended to be a comprehensive guide on the subject of deliverance, nor do we suggest that the church no longer needs experts or deliverance ministries. However, we do believe there are some things we can learn to do ourselves. We should take care of our own daily dental hygiene by brushing our own teeth and flossing, but we still need to go to the dentist for cleanings and dental emergencies.

God has given all believers spiritual weaponry and authority, but many have never been taught how to use their spiritual equipment. When leaders train their congregations to rely on Christ within for daily "spiritual hygiene," they can trust more in God and rely less on other people. As pastors, we rejoice to see Christians in our own fellowship taking personal responsibility for their spiritual growth. As far as we are concerned, it is very fulfilling to serve as coaches equipping the team to "play the game."

SECTION ONE

# TRAINING FOR BATTLE

# Chapter 1

# HITCHHIKERS

## By Dennis

### HUMILIATION

How humiliating! My face flushed red with shame and there was a big lump in my throat. I flung open the front door of my house and sat down heavily on the sofa, burying my face in my hands. Reliving the painful events of the evening was agonizing. A small group of 40 Christians had asked me to share my testimony. Six months earlier I'd been born again, then gloriously filled with the Holy Spirit. The joy was so intense it felt like I'd explode, but it didn't matter. If it killed me, I would be in heaven with Jesus that much sooner. Naturally other believers were excited to hear about what God had done in my life.

The night of the meeting, I was eager to tell others about my powerful, life-changing experience with God. When the worship ended, I was introduced and headed to the lectern. Astoundingly, a feeling of panic gripped me as soon as I walked over to the microphone. What was this? I feared nothing. Or so I thought. My mouth opened, but nothing came out. I stood there in utter shame. My testimony had been so dramatic the whole region was buzzing about it. Now I was unable to say a single word. I couldn't understand what had happened.

After what seemed like an eternity, I turned, walked down the steps of the platform, and sat down. The room was dead silent except for the ticking of a clock. Eventually, the worship leader tried to salvage the evening by giving *her* testimony. I felt wrecked. As soon as the meeting was over I scurried out the nearest exit speaking to no one. What had gone wrong?

## A NEW ANGLE

In the natural, I'd always been a master of bravado, so wimping out now that I was a Christian was repugnant to me. Growing up on the south side of Chicago, I majored in the art of street smarts early on. As a young kid, I walked with the Chicago swagger, appearing tough and menacing on purpose. Scowl and look mean, or you get beat up. Intimidate, and you get what you want. Manipulate successfully, and you win. We tough guys were always "working an angle."

By age ten we could spot the tourists and would hit them up for smokes. Here's a tip. When you go into a big city, don't keep looking up at the skyscrapers. Keep your head down, walk like you are in a hurry, and wear dark clothes so you won't be such an easy mark. Smacking our next victim on the arm, we'd say, "Hey! Give me a cigarette!" Sure enough, their eyes would widen in fear and they'd shove us at least one cigarette, if not the whole pack.

This Christianity stuff was a whole new way of life for me. Before, I had prided myself on my rugged independence. Now, because my surrender to Jesus had been so complete, I found myself living in ever increasing dependence on God. The Lord surprised me with such a powerful immersion in the Holy Spirit and revelation of the Trinity that I was overwhelmed with God and deeply humbled in my own eyes. I quickly learned to come before the Lord like a child, trusting and teachable.

## BURIED ALIVE

Now that I was home, I "inquired of the Lord" like David in the Bible. Sliding to my knees, I prayed, "God, what is wrong with me? I love You and You've changed my whole life. I can feel Your presence, so I know You're with me! So what is going on here?"

In a flash I saw myself in my mind's eye as a nine-year-old boy in bed, with clenched fists, hating myself. I had been a bed-wetter, and that was my secret humiliation. To make it worse, when I finally confided in a friend he let the cat out of the bag, exposing me to all my other buddies.

"What is the matter with me? Why can't I control my own body?" I could feel hatred for myself as well as the shame in my gut. All that anger was still inside me even after twenty years. I was aware that it was wrong to hate people, but now I saw that it was just as sinful to hate myself.

## PARADIGM SHIFT

Along with the anger and shame I felt in my gut, I also felt shame draped over me like a heavy, smothering "blanket." In a flash, I saw myself looking in the mirror but my face was covered by a slimy "stocking mask" with holes for eyes, like the ones burglars wear. Receiving forgiveness from Christ within, the toxic feelings inside me were washed out (see Col. 1:27). Simultaneously I felt a spirit of shame lift off me and saw the mask pulled off in my mind's eye. Instantly the anger and shame were replaced by a deep peace.

> *If we confess our sins, He is faithful and just to forgive us our sins and to cleanse us from all unrighteousness* (1 John 1:9).

We experience emotions *inside* us, in the gut (more about this later). I realized that two things had happened. First, when I received forgiveness God instantly washed out the toxic emotions and replaced them with His peace. Second, because a spirit of shame had been "hitchhiking" on my self-hatred and humiliation, I felt evil *outside* of me. It lifted off me *automatically* when I *let* God deal with the toxic emotions *inside* me. This taught me how to differentiate between internal and external influences.

> *When we forgive, we have peace.*

The Lord taught me two significant lessons through this experience in which I received emotional healing and deliverance simultaneously. I discovered that evil hitchhikers must leave when we deal with our internal issues. In order for a hitchhiker to stay attached to us, they require legal permission. I also learned that I could rely on Jesus the deliverer *in me* for self-deliverance!

> *I AM, I AM the LORD\*! Besides Me there is no Deliverer/ Savior* (Isaiah 43:11 ONMB).[1]

Instead me *doing* deliverance *to* people, I now prefer to teach them how to do *self-deliverance*. Teaching believers how to fish rather than giving them a fish, as the saying goes, helps believers learn to rely on Jesus within. The weekend Jennifer and I first met in 1997, we traveled to Jacksonville, Florida from different states to be intercessors at a conference. Approximately 90 intercessors gathered to pray for Jacksonville. While we were doing "identificational repentance,"[2] a young man began to repent on behalf of those who had become involved with the occult. As he began to pray for witches and warlocks to be saved his face contorted, his voice changed to a growl, and his hands became twisted and claw-like.

Another man and I immediately rushed over and escorted him out of the room. We placed our hands under his arms because he seemed unable to walk in his own power. We essentially carried him along while his feet dragged behind him. The intercessors' room had a series of large windows looking into the hallway. When we exited the room, we looked for a private place to minister to him. We dragged the snarling man one way down the hall. No open rooms. We dragged him in the opposite direction. Every room was locked.

Because of the windows, the intercessors were able to view the entire spectacle as we carried him one way, then the other. We couldn't find a single room that was unlocked, so we finally took him into the men's room. At my instruction, he received forgiveness from Christ in him for engaging in the occult. Then we walked him through the process of yielding to Christ the deliverer within for self-deliverance. In just a short time he was delivered, back in his right mind, and able to return to the group.

*Fear invites evil into our life.*

When believers are equipped for self-deliverance, they are empowered to rely on Christ in them rather than continuously being dependent on others.[3] As believers, we have been given spiritual authority: *"Then the seventy returned with joy, saying, 'Lord, even the demons are subject to us in Your name'"* (Luke 10:17).

> One of the greatest revelations is the revelation of self-deliverance. We can loose ourselves from any control... [of] darkness (Isa. 52:2). We can exercise power and authority for our own lives. Jesus told us to cast out the beam from our own eye (Luke 6:42). The term cast out is the same word used in reference to casting out demons (*ekballō*).[4]

This is not to say that we will never need others to minister to us again. God doesn't let us become completely independent so we don't need any help from one another. However, daily spiritual hygiene can be likened to dental hygiene. We clean our own teeth every day but occasionally must seek the help of a professional. Two instances that usually do require the assistance of other ministers are exceptions, and must be noted—new believers and those who have suffered serious trauma.

## God's In, Evil's Out

Demons cannot remain in a territory ruled by God. We don't stab demons with a sword so they bleed and die. The enemy is *displaced* by the presence of God when He comes in. The Light overcomes darkness. Unforgiveness gives the enemy legal ground to come in, but repentance takes back that ground. Holiness purges out the unclean. God's presence evicts evil and occupies the territory. When God sanctifies an area in our life, His presence takes up residence. He occupies the territory. Demonic hitchhikers are evicted when God enters.

> *When the enemy shall come in like a flood, the Spirit of the Lord will lift up a standard against him and put him to flight* (Isaiah 59:19 AMPC).

When we are first born again and receive forgiveness, God instantly deals with vast areas of our life. However, we don't know how much He dealt with or what remains. It is our responsibility to use what God has given us and cooperate with Him as we grow spiritually.

> *And now, just as you accepted Christ Jesus as your Lord, you must continue to follow him. Let your roots grow down into him, and let your lives be built on him. Then your faith will grow strong in the truth you were taught, and you will overflow with thankfulness* (Colossians 2:6-7 NLT).

## Weapons of Sanctification

To mature spiritually we must learn how to use our "God-tools," also known as *"the weapons of our warfare"* (2 Cor. 10:4), and be diligent in applying them to transform our thoughts, emotions, and impulses (choices) *"into the structure of life shaped by Christ,"* and *"lives of obedience into maturity"* (2 Cor. 10:6 MSG).

> *We use our powerful God-tools for smashing warped philosophies, tearing down barriers erected against the truth of God, fitting every loose thought and emotion and impulse into the structure of life shaped by Christ. Our tools are ready at hand for clearing the ground of every obstruction and building lives of obedience into maturity* (1 Corinthians 10:5-6 MSG).

God created us as thinking, willing, feeling beings. At the time of salvation we experience a great deal of transformation in our thought life, the choices we make, and our emotions. We gain clarity of thought as our hearts turn toward God. Many things that we could not understand before now become clear. Our preferences and actions begin to reflect our desire to love and serve God. We experience supernatural peace with God in our emotions. We are introduced to the fruit of the Spirit at conversion.

At the time of our initial salvation experience, we gain a great deal of freedom. However, many areas of our heart remain "un-evangelized" and don't yet submit to the lordship of Jesus Christ. The good news is that each time we cooperate with God in the ongoing process of sanctification more and more of our heart is set apart for Him. In every area that comes under the authority of God, evil spirits lose their foothold in our life.

> *As you have therefore received Christ, [even] Jesus the Lord, [so] walk* (regulate your lives and conduct yourselves) *in union with and conformity to Him* (Colossians 2:6 AMPC).

> ## *Sanctification is an ongoing process.*

Our initial conversion is instant. *Spiritual growth* is a process. The Lord wants us to *"grow in grace, and in the knowledge of our Lord"* (2 Peter 3:18 KJV). When we are born again, the transformation the Lord desires to accomplish in our life is just beginning. As we pray, study the Scriptures, and apply Christian discipline to our life, we grow in godliness. The word the Bible uses for this process is *sanctification*, which means "set apart for God." *Vine's Expository Dictionary of Old and New Testament Words* defines sanctification as "separation to God" and "the course of life befitting those so separated."[5]

> [Sanctification] must be pursued by the believer, earnestly and undeviatingly.... It is not vicarious, i.e. it cannot be transferred or imputed...[but] built up, little by little, as the result of obedience to the Word of God, and of following the example of Christ...in the power of the Holy Spirit.[6]

> ## *Spiritual growth is a process.*

## BACK TO THE GARDEN

When Adam and Eve lived in the Garden of Eden, prior to sin entering the picture, they had perfect harmony with God and one another. The only emotions they felt were God's emotions. Emotions were created to be conduits, or "pipes," for the love of God. We experience the love of God as the fruit of the Spirit—one fruit, multiple functions (see Gal. 5:22-23).

- Joy is love rejoicing (finding deep pleasure in God's presence).

- Peace is love resting (having an assurance that everything is in God's hands).

- Patience is love enduring (willing to wait for God's timing).

- Kindness is love giving (serving others with mercy).

- Goodness is love motivating (love and holiness).

- Faith is love trusting (we can believe God and others can believe us).

- Gentleness is love esteeming ("esteem others better" than yourself, see Phil. 2:3).

- Self-control is love restraining (power under control).

As soon as sin entered the picture, Adam and Eve were catapulted into a kingdom of disharmony, toxic emotions, and evil tormentors. In just a few short verses of Scripture, Adam and Eve felt hurt, fear, lust, anger, guilt, and shame for the first time (see Gen 3:1–24).[7] Every negative emotion signals an area where the enemy has legal ground. The banner over the kingdom of God is love (see Song of Sol. 2:4). The flag over the kingdom of the devil is fear. God's emotions are *love-based* while negative emotions are *fear-based*.

> **God's emotions are love-based.**
> **Negative emotions are fear-based.**

When we become a believer, we are rescued out of the kingdom of the enemy and gain access to God's kingdom. God *"delivered us from the power of darkness and conveyed us into the kingdom of the Son of His love"* (Col. 1:13). In the seven messages to the churches in the Book of Revelation, Jesus promises access to a spiritual Garden of Eden in the kingdom of God to those who overcome. We have inherited all that Adam and Eve forfeited. However, we must *appropriate* our inheritance or it's like unclaimed money in the bank.

> *He who has an ear, let him hear what the Spirit says to the churches. To him who overcomes I will give to eat from the tree of life, which is in the midst of the Paradise of God* (Revelation 2:7).

## FORGIVENESS IS THE KEY

The Bible tells us that we must still deal with two spiritual kingdoms even though we are saved (see 1 Pet. 5:8; Eph. 6:11). Christians are the property of God. The only way evil spirits can harass and torment us is when we give the enemy permission. As long as demons have a legal right in us, they can either refuse to leave or come right back even after we try to cast them off. Negative emotions always give the enemy permission to harass us. This is the major source of unnecessary trouble and torment in the lives of believers.

> *Like a flitting sparrow, like a flying swallow, so a curse without cause shall not alight* (Proverbs 26:2).

*Negative emotions remove us from God's protection.*

Emotions are signals that let us know what kingdom is in operation at any given time. Negative emotions let us know that we are temporarily under the sway of the wrong kingdom. Just as forgiveness transported us into the kingdom of God at the time of salvation, forgiveness is the answer for all negative emotions. Forgiveness always gets us back to God's territory. When we forgive, we are instantly restored to the supernatural peace of God. Peace is the evidence that nothing is separating us from the presence of God.

> *Emotions show us what*
> *kingdom we're in.*

## IT'S SIMPLE FOR GOD

Sin may be complicated, but God's remedy is simple. The solution for freedom in every instance is applying forgiveness and repentance. Properly applied, forgiveness takes back legal ground from the enemy every time and "sets that area apart" for God, or *sanctifies* the areas that were once in enemy hands. Evil can't touch something God controls.

Common ways in which the enemy gets a foothold are:

- Unforgiveness

- Emotional trauma

- Physical abuse

- Sexual abuse

- Mental strongholds

- Repetitive sin

- Generational sin

- Sexual sin

- Unhealthy soul ties

- Idolatry (and agendas)

- Religion (religious spirits)

- Occult activity

> *Evil can't touch something*
> *God controls.*

The erroneous belief that forgiveness is a long and difficult process is widely accepted. Others wrongly think that forgiveness is just an act of the will but you have to live with the pain. True forgiveness must include the mind, the will, *and* the emotions. We know forgiveness has been accomplished when a toxic emotion changes to peace. It is a supernatural exchange. Forgiveness is always instant, just like it was when we first got saved, and washes out negative emotions completely.

> *Forgiveness is instant!*

We are admonished to be diligent in our pursuit of God. That includes cleaning out toxic emotions...on a daily basis! Don't *"let the sun go down on your wrath"* (Eph. 4:26). When God placed Adam and Eve in the Garden of Eden, He assigned them the work of tending the garden. In the same way, we have each been given the task of caring for the garden of our own heart.

At first our lives are like an overgrown plot of land filled with briars and dead branches. When we are "purchased by God" He begins the work of making something beautiful out of the mess we've made of our life. However, we must do our part.

Some individuals have a faulty theology that the Lord will *sovereignly* set us free from negative emotions whenever *He* decides to act. Unforgiveness is sin. Should we continue in sin and passively wait to be delivered by God as a sovereign work? Of course not! The Scriptures clearly tell us to obey God. We are commanded to forgive (see Matt. 6:15). Therefore we must take responsibility for what we allow to remain in our heart.

We should keep short accounts with God. In accounting, keeping our accounts on a *short basis* means to not let them become extended. We stay "paid up." Like David, we must invite the Lord to search our heart on a regular basis (see Ps. 139:23-24). He can't deal with something we don't present to Him.

> *Therefore, my dear ones…work out* (cultivate, carry out to the goal, and fully complete) *your own salvation with reverence and awe and trembling* (Philippians 2:12 AMPC).

### *Keep short accounts with God.*

Toxic emotions are always the product of unforgiveness. The Bible commands us to forgive, so when we don't forgive we are disobedient to God. Allowing negative emotions to fester in our heart because we won't allow forgiveness to wash them out is clearly wrong. Should we keep on sinning and wait until God acts, or should we simply be obedient to the Word of God? The Lord won't violate our will. He won't *make* us do what is right. We must choose to obey.

## TAKE BACK GROUND

This side of heaven, the Lord is continually working on us (see Jer. 18:2–4). I approach God for cleansing even when nothing negative is manifesting outwardly. We call this process "intentional sanctification." Rather than waiting for a crisis, we present our hearts to the Lord for cleansing on a regular basis. David, a man after God's own heart, asked the Lord to search his heart for *secret* faults about which David himself was unaware. He practiced a humility we all should emulate. After all, only God can know the entirety of our heart.

*Who can discern his lapses and errors? Clear me from hidden [and unconscious] faults* (Psalm 19:12 AMPC).

---

### *Unforgiveness is sin.*

---

Jesus says, *"If you have anything against anyone, forgive him, that your Father in heaven may also forgive you your trespasses. But if you do not forgive, neither will your Father in heaven forgive your trespasses"* (Mark 11:25-26). This does not mean we lose our salvation if we fail to forgive someone, but we will suffer the consequences of our sin and will be turned over to tormenting demonic harassment (see Matt. 18:21–35).

Our conscious mind only knows a tiny portion of all that is hidden within us. Even when we can't think of anything, the Lord will reveal what needs to be dealt with when we get in an attitude of prayer. When we ask God to show us secret sins and issues in our heart, the Lord is always faithful. Never once has He said, "You are now perfect and have no need of Me!"

*Search me, O God, and know my heart; try me and know my anxious thoughts; and see if there be any hurtful way in me, and lead me in the everlasting way* (Psalm 139:23-24 NASB).

The principles for forgiveness, emotional healing, bringing down strongholds, and self-deliverance can be easily learned and quickly applied by all believers, including young children. We have taught many children as young as three and four years old to forgive and let Jesus wash "bad feelings" out. Children actually learn more easily than adults because they haven't spent years living by willpower and intellect. God has equipped all Christians, young and old, with the tools for victorious Christian living.

> *God has equipped all*
> *Christians for victory!*

## NOTES

1.  "The One New Man Bible uses LORD* to translate the Tetragrammaton, the four letter name of God. The name is a Hebrew word meaning, "I was, I AM, I always will be." He never changes. In the New Testament there is a problem because the authors of the Septuagint used the same Greek word, Kurios, that the authors of the New Testament used to translate the name of God, which is always translated in English as Lord. In the New Testament the word Kurios is used in reference to both Y'shua or to the LORD* when quoting or alluding to the LORD* in Hebrew Scripture. There is no distinction in the Greek text between the word Lord in reference to Y'shua or to the LORD*." Therefore, in the One New Man Bible, I AM is always translated as LORD* to make a differentiation. W.J. Morford, *One New Man Bible* (Traveler's Rest, SC: True Potential Publishing, Inc., 2011). ii.

2.  Identificational repentance is a type of prayer in which one or more individuals confess the corporate sins of a nation, group of people, race, church, family, and so forth. J. Dawson, *Healing America's Wounds,* (Ventura, CA: Regal House Publishing, 1994), 15; C. Jacobs, *Possessing the Gates of the Enemy,* (Tarrytown, NY: Fleming H. Revell Publishing, 1991), 192, 236; C. Peter Wagner, *Praying with Power,* (Ventura, CA: Regal House Publishing, 1997), 95.

3.  F. Hammond and I. Hammond, *Pigs in the Parlor,* (Kirkwood, MO: Impact Christian Books, Inc. 2010), 69.

4.   J. Eckhardt, *Deliverance and Spiritual Warfare Manual: A Comprehensive Guide to Living Free,* (Lake Mary, FL: Charisma House, 2014), 33.

5.   "Sanctify" is *hagiazo* in Greek, meaning *consecrate, dedicate, purify, or separate unto God.* The English word *sanctification* comes from the Greek root *hagios* meaning "holy," referring to holiness in moral with divine qualities superior to human nature, which is Christlikeness. "Sanctification is...used in the New Testament...of the separation of the believer from evil things and evil ways. This sanctification is God's will for the believer, 1 Thess. 4:3, and His purpose in calling him by the gospel, ver. 7; it must be learned from God, ver. 4, as He teaches it by His Word, John 17:17, 19; cp. Ps. 17:4; 119:9.... The Holy Spirit is the Agent of sanctification...." W.E. Vine, *Vine's Expository Dictionary of Old and New Testament Words* (Fleming H. Revell Company, 1981). V. 3, 315.

6.   Ibid.

7.   In the Garden of Eden, before Adam and Eve sinned, they only experienced the love, joy, and peace of God—God's emotions—in their emotions. Our emotions are like "pipes" God created to transmit the flow of His love. Before they sinned, Adam and Eve only felt love in their emotions. Emotions were created to be conduits of the love of God. The fruit of the Spirit listed in Galatians 5:22-23 describe functions of the love of God.

Because Adam had sinned, his spirit was separated from God. He died a spiritual death. Harmony between God and man was fractured. Adam became ruled by flesh instead of God's Spirit. Man's fallen nature and God's heavenly nature were no longer in alignment. Adam's thoughts, choices, and emotions—in his soul—were now carnal or fleshly. Adam and Eve now experienced negative emotions for the first time. They felt hurt, lust, anger, guilt, and shame— emotions from hell that gave the enemy permission to torment them. Sickness and disease entered their lives at the same time.

When a believer yields to God, they experience God's emotions as the fruit of the Spirit. When a Christian fails to yield, they experience carnal emotions. Our emotions sound the alarm and let us know whether the kingdom of God is ruling or the kingdom of the enemy.

When we experience the peace of God, it means the Prince of Peace is ruling in our heart. Negative emotions mean that the enemy has taken some ground. How do you know if you have encountered territory taken by the enemy? Negative emotions. How do you know if you are territory ruled by God? God's emotions—the fruit of the Spirit!

*Chapter 2*

# Spiritual Real Estate

## By Dr. Jen

Jesus Himself is our example of what it means to be *fully human* according to God's design. Normal Christianity begins in a place of victory because of the finished work of Jesus. Anything less is not "normal" but *sub-normal* Christianity.

> What is the normal Christian life? We do well at the outset to ponder this question. It is something very different from the life of the average Christian. Indeed a consideration of the written Word of God—of the Sermon on the Mount for example—should lead us to ask whether such a life has ever in fact been lived upon the earth, save only by the Son of God Himself. But in that last saving clause lies immediately the answer to our question.
>
> The Apostle Paul gives us his own definition of the Christian life in Galatians 2:20. It is "no longer I, but Christ". Here he is not stating something special or peculiar—a

high level of Christianity. He is...presenting God's normal for a Christian, which can be summarized in the words: I live no longer, but Christ lives His life in me. God makes it quite clear in His Word that He has only one answer to every human need—His Son, Jesus Christ. In all His dealings with us He works by taking us out of the way and substituting Christ in our place. The Son of God died instead of us for our forgiveness: He lives instead of us for our deliverance.[1]

How then can we possibly live a normal Christian life? The good news is that we need nothing more than what we already possess to be triumphant. However, it is essential to understand the location of our spiritual "real estate" and how to use the spiritual equipment, or God-tools, that God has given us in order to grow to maturity, *"to a perfect [mature] man, to the measure of the stature of the fullness of Christ"* (Eph. 4:13).

Dennis and I spent years in itinerant ministry going from church to church. We were dismayed when we discovered that approximately 90 percent of believers don't know where their will and emotions are located, how to yield to Christ within, or even how to forgive. If we don't know where our will is, how can we surrender our will to God's will? If we don't know where our emotions are centered, how can we present them to Christ for healing when we are emotionally wounded? If we don't know *how* to forgive, how can we obey Jesus's command *to* forgive? How can we close doors that give the enemy permission to torment us?

The number one principle of real estate is location, location, location. The first essential lesson we must learn for effective Christian living is also location! It is vital for us to identify the location of our spiritual real estate. Let's take a look at what the Bible says.

## LOCATION OF OUR HEART

The Feast of Tabernacles is an eight-day festival to thank God for His bounty and ask Him to provide rain for the crops in the coming year. It is one of the three feasts that Jews were to observe each year by going to Jerusalem to *"appear before the Lord your God in the place which He chooses"* (Deut. 16:16).

The Gospel of John records that Jesus not only went up to Jerusalem to celebrate the festival but used water, a symbol from the Feast of Tabernacles celebration, to represent who He is and what He offers to believers. On the last day of the Feast, Jesus cried out with a loud voice, promising the gift of the outpouring of the Holy Spirit.

> *In the last day, that great day of the feast, Jesus stood and cried, saying, If any man thirst, let him come unto me, and drink. He that believeth on me, as the scripture hath said, out of his belly shall flow rivers of living water.* (But this spake He of the Spirit, which they that believe on him should receive: for the Holy Ghost was not yet given; because that Jesus was not yet glorified) (John 7:37–39 KJV).

This promised outflow seems surprising in two particular ways. First, the rivers would flow out of the hearts of individual believers to others and the world. Second, the source out of which the living waters flow, the "belly," is the literal meaning of the original Greek word *koilia*.

> That immediately confronts us with the strangeness of the source of the Holy Spirit. The source is our belly. You would not expect that. You would expect that Jesus would have said something like this: Out of his mouth, or out of his heart, or out of his mind, or out of his soul, will flow these rivers of living water. But, no, out of his belly. Christ spoke here as a good Hebrew. The Hebrews of the Old Testament regarded the bowels, located deep in the belly,

as the location of the experience of the child of God. That carried over in passages of the Bible that speak of "bowels of compassion." Oh, when somebody dear to us, say a son or a daughter, is in deep trouble, deep distress, then a parent feels that trouble and his compassion for that child, deep down in the stomach, in the bowels, in the belly. We receive salvation in our heart. We know salvation with our mind. We experience salvation in our belly.[2]

> *We receive salvation in our heart.*
> *We know salvation with our mind.*
> *We experience salvation in our belly.*

### Old Testament

Only when we locate our spirit-heart correctly can we effectively *guard our heart*. Proverbs 4:23 tells us *"out of it spring the issues of life."* The heart is the center of man's inward life and the sphere of divine influence. Whenever the Bible talks about the heart as our innermost being, it is not referring to the chest or physical heart.

The most common word for "heart" in the Old Testament is the Hebrew word *leb* (*lev*) or *lebab* (*levav*), which is translated "heart" in this verse of Scripture. It occurs almost 600 times in the Old Testament. The term *leb* is very general, referring to many aspects of our being including our innermost being, will, inclinations, understanding, soul, memory, passions, and resolve.

> *Love the Lord your God with all your heart [Hebrew: lev], with all your soul, and with all your strength* (Deuteronomy 6:5).

However, other words are also used specifically indicating that the location of the heart is in the belly. *Me'ah,* Strong's #4578, translated figuratively as "heart," literally means intestines, abdomen, belly; also stomach, womb (or for men, the seat of generation), belly, and bowels.

> *I delight to do thy will, O my God: yea, thy law is within my heart [Hebrew: me'ah]* (Psalm 40:8 KJV).

> *I am poured out like water, and all my bones are out of joint: my heart [lev] is like wax; it is melted in the midst of my bowels [Hebrew: me'ah]* (Psalm 22:14 KJV).

The Jews correctly regarded the gut as the seat of tender affections, particularly kindness, benevolence, and compassion but also passion, mourning, and suffering. Another word used to refer to the heart is *beten*, literally meaning belly, abdomen, inward parts, womb, and sometimes the seat of physical hunger but also used figuratively for innermost being or heart.

> *The words of a talebearer are as wounds, and they go down into the innermost parts of the belly [Hebrew: beten, belly, abdomen, womb, inner man, heart]* (Proverbs 18:8 KJV).

### New Testament

In the New Testament, the heart, at our core or mid-section, is also where our conscience resides, together with the epicenter of our emotions, moral nature, and spiritual life—which, as in John 7:38, flows out of the "belly" or *koilia* in the original Greek. *Koilia*'s literal meaning is belly, abdomen, bowels, stomach, and womb. Figuratively, *koilia* refers to the innermost being or heart.

*Splanchnon*, used nine times in the New Testament, is also translated at times "heart." The literal meaning is inward parts, innards, viscera, intestines, and womb, and, figuratively, compassion, affections, and the seat of the emotions.

The Greek word *kardia*, meaning "heart," can mean either the figurative heart or physical heart. In the New Testament, however, *kardia* is used 159 times for our emotional and spiritual center, but is used literally in only a single verse of Scripture which refers to physical death caused by fear: *"Men's hearts failing them from fear and the expectation of those things...coming on the earth"* (Luke 21:26).[3]

> *He that believeth on me, as the scripture hath said, out of his belly [Greek: koilia, belly, abdomen, womb, inner man] shall flow rivers of living water* (John 7:38 KJV).

> *But whoso hath this world's good, and seeth his brother have need, and shutteth up his bowels of compassion [Greek: splanchnon, intestines, affection, compassion, tender mercies] from him, how dwelleth the love of God in him?* (1 John 3:17 KJV).

> *For God is my record, how greatly I long after you all in the bowels [Greek: splanchnon, intestines, affection, compassion, tender mercies] of Jesus Christ* (Philippians 1:8 KJV).

> *Let not your heart [Greek: kardia, the center of man's inward life] be troubled; ye believe in God, believe also in me* (John 14:1 KJV).

It is important to note that our human spirit is not located in an actual physical organ of the body. Our spirit is not physical matter or energy (a form of matter) such as chemical, electrical, or thermal energy. The Bible tells us a spiritual realm exists, God is Spirit (see John 4:24), angels are spirits (see Heb. 1:13-14), and we are spirit beings in a material body. We can only know and worship God by approaching Him spirit-to-Spirit.

> *God is Spirit, and those who worship Him must worship in spirit and truth* (John 4:24).

## BIBLE HEART

We use the term *Bible heart* to specify our heart as defined by the Bible. When you got saved, did you ask Jesus into your head? That question always gets a smile or a chuckle. Believers know intuitively that salvation takes place in the *heart*! We must believe in our *heart* to be saved (see Rom. 10:9). We must also forgive from our *heart* (see Matt. 18:35). "From the heart" is the key. Our inner reality is determined by what is in our heart, not by the words we say or our mental analysis. What happens in our heart is what counts.

Our spirit fills us from head to toe. However, the *epicenter* of our spirit resides in our belly. The anointing from Christ within flows out from our belly.

*The spirit of man is centered in the belly.*

> *The spirit of man is the candle of the Lord, searching all the inward parts of the **belly*** (Proverbs 20:27 KJV).

*The anointing from Christ within flows from the belly.*

> *He that believeth on me, as the scripture hath said, out of his **belly** shall flow rivers of living water* (John 7:38 KJV).

*Love and compassion flow from the belly.*

> *Joseph made haste; for his bowels did yearn upon his brother: and he sought where to weep; and he entered into his chamber, and wept there* (Genesis 43:30 KJV).

> *Mine eyes do fail with tears, my bowels are troubled* (Lamentations 2:11a KJV).

> *For God is my record, how greatly I long after you all in the bowels [affection] of Jesus Christ* (Philippians 1:8 KJV).

## DOOR OF THE HEART

Our human spirit fills us head to toe, but we connect with our spirit through our heart's *door*. Our heart is the epicenter of emotional and spiritual activity and, based on what the Scriptures tell us, through it alone can we connect with the realm of the spirit. Jesus says He knocks at our heart's door but waits for us to open to Him.

> *Behold, I stand at the door and knock. If anyone hears My voice and opens the door, I will come in to him and dine with him, and he with Me* (Revelation 3:20).

Christianity is spiritual relationship, and we can have relationship only with those to whom our heart is open. We call the heart of man, as defined by Scripture, by the term "Bible heart" to distinguish it from our physical heart.

## WHAT HAPPENS IN OUR HEART?

Jonathan Edwards (1703–1758)—preacher, theologian, missionary to Native Americans, and father of the First Great Awakening in America—addressed the question of head versus heart Christianity, which was a major doctrinal dispute among the clergy of that day.[4] Contrary to the view of many preachers and theologians, Edwards insisted that the emotions are the *gateway* to knowing God. He doubted the reality of a salvation experience unless the emotions were deeply impacted.[5]

Ironically, this question is already clearly settled in the Scriptures. Real Christianity is a matter of the heart not the head. It is a relationship rather than a philosophy.

Within our heart, we find:

- the seat of grief (see John 14:1; Rom. 9:2; 2 Cor. 2:4)

- joy (see John 16:22; Eph. 5:19)

- the desires (see Matt. 5:28; 2 Pet. 2:14)

- the affections (see Luke 24:32; Acts 21:13)

- the perceptions (see John 12:40; Eph. 4:18)

- the thoughts (see Matt. 9:4; Heb. 4:12)

- the understanding (see Matt. 13:15; Rom. 1:21)

- the reasoning powers (see Mark 2:6; Luke 24:38)

- the imagination (see Luke 1:51)

- the conscience (see Acts 2:37; 1 John 3:20)

- the intentions (see Heb. 4:12; 1 Pet. 4:1)

- purpose (see Acts 11:23; 2 Cor. 9:7)

- the will or volition (see Rom. 6:17; Col. 3:15)

- faith (see Mark 11:23; Rom. 10:10; Heb. 3:12)

It is apparent, therefore, that our heart is the center of our emotional and spiritual life. Jesus says, *"He that believeth on me, as the scripture hath said, out of his **belly** shall flow rivers of living water"* (John 7:38 KJV). All spiritual reality is a matter of the heart.

Salvation takes place only when we open our heart to Jesus and receive Him. We must "believe in our heart" to be saved (see Rom. 10:9). For forgiveness to be acceptable to God, we must forgive from our *heart* (see Matt. 18:35).

> *All spiritual reality is a*
> *matter of the heart.*

## NOTES

1. W. Nee, *The Normal Christian Life*, (Memphis, TN: Bottom of the Hill Publishing, 2014), 5.

2. D. Engelsma, "Out-flowing Spirit of Jesus," *The Standard Bearer* (vol. 88, Issue 16, May 15, 2012). Preached Pentecost Sunday 2011. Retrieved September 18, 2013 from the official website of Protestant Reformed Churches in America http://www.prca.org/resources/publications/articles/ item/3639-out-flowing-spirit-of-jesus-a-pentecost-sermon.

3. Assuming that the physical heart is the site of spiritual and emotional activity is a common misconception. Whenever the Bible talks about the heart, it is not referring to either the chest area or the physical heart that pumps our blood. The only time the New Testament refers to the physical heart is in Luke 21:26, where Jesus prophesies that, in the end times, terrible distress of nations will cause "men's hearts" to fail them from fear. Dennis and I use the term "Bible heart" for the emotional/spiritual heart to distinguish it from the physical heart.

4. "How do we discern between true religion, and false? In this classic treatise on the nature of authentic faith, enormously influential American preacher and theologian Jonathan Edwards (1703–1758) explores the difference between true and counterfeit religious experiences, and how deep and sincere emotion can accentuate a real connection to God." J. Edwards, *A Treatise Concerning Religious Affections,* (New York: Cosimo Classics, 2007).

5. Ibid., 23–25.

*Chapter 3*

# SEAT OF THE EMOTIONS

## BY DR. JEN

The devil doesn't take time off and neither should Christians. Ephesians chapter six tells us to be prepared at all times so we don't get ambushed by the enemy: *"Be strong in the Lord and in the power of His might. Put on the whole armor of God, that you may be able to stand against the wiles of the devil"* (Eph. 6:10-11).

Because we are called to live our faith 24/7, Christianity is a step-by-step proposition. In Bible times, the shoes of Roman soldiers were a vital foundation of their armament. Not only was walking their main means of "transportation," they required footwear that could provide solid positioning in the heat of battle. The sandals of a Roman soldier were designed for marching, fighting, and standing for long periods of time. The soles were thick leather studded with iron hobnails, giving them a firm footing in battle.

The apostle Paul tells us to wear *shoes of peace* as part of our armor. Peace is not just tranquility but the power of God to maintain a victorious stance. Peace is militant, and the enemy cannot prevail against it. The *"God of peace will crush Satan under your feet"* (Rom. 16:20). Because Jesus Himself is our peace, when *we* have peace the enemy can't touch us (see Eph. 2:14).

> *For shoes, put on the peace that comes from the Good News so that you will be fully prepared* (Ephesians 6:15 NLT).

Therefore, unless we learn to deal with our emotions we will have a difficult time living our Christianity because emotions are the key to it all. When the Lord took Dennis to the school of the Spirit, He taught him that an abiding lifestyle was possible only when we tap into the fruit of the Spirit as a continual practice (see John 15:5). When we abide, we are in the presence of God and peace is evidence of His presence.

Jesus gave us the gift of supernatural peace so it is possible to live in peace continually (see John 14:27). We can move away from His presence and get in the flesh, but He never leaves us: *"I will never leave you nor forsake you"* (Heb. 13:5).

Dennis discovered that any negative emotion separated him from peace and therefore the tangible presence of the Lord. However, he discovered that anything toxic he felt was quickly washed out when forgiveness was applied in his heart. As soon as his heart was cleansed, peace was instantly restored. The Lord told Dennis, "Don't let anything come between what you and I have together!" No matter how chaotic the external circumstances of life may become, the peace of God is always available to guard us (see Phil. 4:7).

## FUNCTIONS OF THE HEART

All spiritual reality is a matter of the *heart,* not the head. No wonder we are admonished to pay careful attention to what goes on in our heart (see Prov. 4:23). According to the Scriptures:

- Salvation happens in the heart.

*For with the **heart** one believes unto righteousness, and with the mouth confession is made unto salvation* (Romans 10:10).

- Faith resides in the heart.
  *Let us draw near with a true **heart** in full assurance of faith* (Hebrews 10:22a).

- We trust God in the heart.
  *Trust in the Lord with all your **heart*** (Proverbs 3:5a).

- The Word of God is planted in the heart.
  *The sower sows the word. And these are the ones by the wayside where the word is sown. When they hear, Satan comes immediately and takes away the word that was sown in their **hearts*** (Mark 4:14-15).

- True forgiveness comes from the heart.
  *This is how my heavenly Father will treat each of you unless you forgive...from your **heart*** (Matthew 18:35 NIV).

- Christian fellowship is a matter of the heart.
  *Finally, all of you be of one mind, having compassion for one another; love as brothers, be **tenderhearted*** (1 Peter 3:8).

## HEAD-HEART CONNECTION

Children often get tummy aches when they have emotional pain. We can feel "butterflies" in our tummy because of anticipation or excitement. We usually make wiser decisions when we follow our heart rather than relying upon logical reasoning alone. Policemen and firefighters learn to "go with their gut" on their job.

Our heart often knows more than our head!

## We have feeling-thoughts.

Scientific studies demonstrate that we have an emotional "brain" in our gut that is as active and important as the brain between our ears. It is called the "second brain." Dr. Michael Gershon, researcher in the field of gastroenterology, published his groundbreaking book on this subject in 1999, and it caused a tectonic shift in the biological sciences.[1] The second brain is our *enteric nervous system*.[2]

Experts in neurobiology and psychotherapy have defined a new field of research—*neurogastroenterology,* or "enteric neurology." Although we have a brain between our ears, God has given us a "second brain" with an equally significant function of emotional cognition, or *knowing*, in our gut. Have you ever heard anyone use the expression "I *know* that I know"? There are two places of knowing—head and heart.

Our two brains are connected by the left vagus nerve, which travels from the emotional center in the brain (limbic system) directly to the intestines. (Emotional information is also transmitted directly to the cells via neuropeptides, or "molecules of emotion.")[3] The left vagus nerve primarily transmits emotional information *from the gut* to the brain, not the other way around.

Our gut tells our brain how we feel![4]

We instantly feel an emotion when we *think* about a painful experience. Our two "brains" experience the memory at the same time. We have *feeling-thoughts,* or "emo-cognitions," and *feeling-choices,* "emo-volition." Emotions rule both our thoughts and choices. It's a closed feedback loop that functions automatically...unless something from the outside breaks into the loop. When we pray, we allow God into the loop, and He changes us on the inside.[5]

> *We have feeling-choices.*

Romans chapter seven describes the fierce inner battle that takes place within the loop when God isn't ruling:

> *I've tried everything and nothing helps. I'm at the end of my rope. Is there no one who can do anything for me? Isn't that the real question? The answer, thank God, is that Jesus Christ can and does. He acted to set things right in this life of contradictions where I want to serve God with all my heart and mind, but am pulled by the influence of sin to do something totally different* (Romans 7:24-25 MSG).

Where does this battle come from in the life of a believer? Our hidden toxic emotions cause ongoing cycles of trouble that happen over and over again. Most of the roots are hidden or forgotten in the subconscious part of us. Our conscious mind is like a bucket of sand, but our subconscious is like the rest of the sand on the whole beach. We can't figure it out. That's why David asked God to search him for faults hidden in the loop so they wouldn't control him.

> *How can I know all the sins lurking in my heart? Cleanse me from these hidden faults. ...Don't let them control me* (Psalm 19:12-13 NLT).

> *All spiritual reality is a matter of the heart.*

David prayed, *"Search me, O God, and know my heart; try me and know my anxious thoughts; and see if there be any hurtful way in me, and lead me in the everlasting way"* (Ps. 139:23-24 NASB). Notice that David speaks of "thoughts that are anxious" and "ways that are hurtful." The Bible shows this clear interweaving of our heart, tying together emotional thoughts and our emotional choices.

> The evidence has been piling up throughout history, and now neuroscientists have proved it's true: The brain's wiring emphatically relies on emotion over intellect in decision-making.... In fact, people who lack emotions because of brain injuries often have difficulty making decisions at all.... The brain stores emotional memories of past decisions, and those are what drive people's choices in life.... [Neuroscientist Antonio Damasio] says: "What makes you and me 'rational' is not suppressing our emotions, but tempering them in a positive way."[6]

*The brain relies on emotion over intellect.*

## "Bucket Man"

A number of years ago I made a "bucket man" poster as a visual aid for Sunday school. A picture of a crank with rope wrapped around it with a hole in the middle is over "bucket man's" head. A piece of string is threaded through the hole and tied to a cardboard bucket with a pipe cleaner handle. When the bucket goes down, blue cardboard "water" is Velcroed to the bucket to represent living water. When the bucket goes up to bucket man's head, the water is removed.

Focus is like a spiritual "bucket" inside. When we open the door of our heart to God, our bucket drops down to the fountain of living water in our heart. However, when we focus on our intellect, we pull our bucket back up to our head. A young child commented, "There's no living water in our head!" The children love the bucket man illustration, but it helps adults catch on as well.

*Counsel in the heart of man is like water in a deep well, but a man of understanding draws it out* (Proverbs 20:5 AMPC).

*Whoever drinks of the water that I shall give him will never thirst. But the water that I shall give him will become in him a fountain of water springing up into everlasting life* (John 4:14).

### When we pray, God gets in the loop.

As soon as we drop down to our spirit and include the Lord, we should feel a gentle awareness that He is with us. We experience the peace of His presence. It is much the same as driving a car with a passenger in the back seat. You may not be able to see them, but you know they are there. When Dennis was teaching me about peace and the presence of God, he reminded me to "include God" in the moment. Whenever I felt troubled, I realized that I was relying on myself rather than God. As soon as I transferred my trust to God, I could feel a gentle sense of calmness and an assurance that God was with me.

When I first started praying with Dennis in the morning, I was like a yoyo—up and down, up and down. Keeping my hand on my belly reminded me to focus on Christ within instead of my thoughts. As I truly began living in the reality that He is *always* with me, it was life changing. I learned that distance is a deception. The Lord is not just far away in heaven but *with us* in our heart. We are God indwelt— *Christ in us, our hope of glory* (see Col. 1:27).

## ABIDING IN THE VINE

As we learn to stay connected to the Lord during our daily activities, we "practice the presence of God."[7] We begin to *abide* in the vine when we stay connected to Christ within even while our eyes are open (see John 15:5).

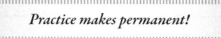

*Practice makes permanent!*

Peace can seem very gentle and subtle. Don't expect lightning bolts or euphoria. Small children may use the word "good" to describe peace. Even if you only feel a mild sense of well-being, as long as you are aware of Christ within, that is the peace of His presence. The more yielded we become, the more peace we feel.

If you become distracted during the day and disconnect, don't become frustrated with yourself. Simply make the connection again. Remember, practice makes...permanent.

For God to work in us we must first yield our will to allow God's will to rule. We engage in the process with God—yielding is active. It is a merging of wills—our will and God's melt together as one. When we yield to Him, the Lord empowers us. Just as we respond to a yield sign while driving a car—we slow down and allow someone else to have the right of way—so we yield our will to God and let Him work. We allow Him to rule in our hearts through peace. We enter into a romance of wills—God's and mine.

*It is a romance of wills—*
*God's and mine.*

Philippians 2:13 tells us: *"It is God who works in you both **to will** and **to do** for His good pleasure."* When we yield our will to God's will, He works. Instead of *trying* to feel something or make something happen, simply surrender to God's presence within.

## LEARNING TO WAIT

Peace is the *starting place* for living the Christian life. The Scriptures command us to *"let the peace of God rule"* in our life (Col. 3:15). When we let go, God takes over.

> *Peace is the starting place to live the Christian life.*

Most supernatural peace is too quiet for our flesh. Therefore, we must *learn* to be still. Psalm 46:10 commands us: *"Be still, and know that I am God."* "Be still," *rapha,* means "let go, surrender, or release." God doesn't become louder; we must become quieter.

> *Surely I have calmed and quieted my soul, like a weaned child with his mother; like a weaned child is my soul within me* (Psalm 131:2).

Although some individuals may instantly feel the presence of God strongly when they drop down to their spirit, the sense of His presence will increase over time for all. The absence of turmoil is a good starting point, but your awareness of God's presence will grow when you continue the practice of yielding to Messiah within. Therefore, we must become still to hear from the Lord and enjoy His presence.

> *When we let go, God takes over!*

**Practice**

Sit down in a quiet room and close your eyes. Place your hand on your belly. Relax and yield to Messiah in you. Focus on your heart. You become more aware of the Lord when you pay attention to Him.

Honor God by acknowledging the fact that He is with you. The Lord is not only omnipresent but you are also God-indwelt.

Spend a few minutes waiting in the presence of God. Often, as we become more relaxed, our awareness of peace increases.

NOTE: We shouldn't ever attempt to make our mind go blank, but simply become aware that the Lord is with us by paying attention to Him. Focus is the opposite of "blank."

## WOUNDS OF THE HEART

Wounds of the heart manifest as negative emotions and are centered in the belly. Even if we feel a lump in the throat or an upset stomach due to toxic emotions, it starts in the gut. They come to the surface every time the people and circumstances of life trigger them. Negative emotions remain in the heart until they are removed by forgiveness. Even if we forget about them, they are still there. Emotions don't die; we bury them alive!

> *The words of a talebearer are as wounds, and they go down into the innermost parts of the **belly*** (Proverbs 18:8 KJV).

> *My **bowels** boiled, and rested not: the days of affliction prevented me* (Job 30:27 KJV).

> *Emotions don't die; we*
> *bury them alive!*

The kingdom of God is described in terms of emotions: *"The kingdom of God is...righteousness* [love in action] *and peace and joy in the Holy Spirit*" (Rom. 14:17). When we feel the peace of God, we are safe. It means the Prince of Peace is ruling and the enemy can't touch us. However, as mentioned previously, toxic emotions are warning signals alerting us to danger. They let us know which kingdom is ruling moment by moment.

The Golan Heights in Israel has national parks and nature trails that attract many tourists to the area. Because much of the land is not arable, tourism generates much-needed income to the Israeli settlements there. However, some sections are fenced off and have clearly marked signs to warn hikers about land mines which were planted there during previous wars.

When we have multiple unresolved issues, life is full of hidden emotional "land mines." In the natural, land mines explode only once. Toxic emotions, on the other hand, explode repeatedly until they are removed by forgiveness. Toxic emotions warn us that we have entered a mine field.

Right after Dennis and I got married, he prayed with me on a regular basis for approximately two months using the principles found in this book. It changed my life forever. Although I once felt "under attack" on a regular basis, after I let the Lord cleanse my heart skirmishes with the enemy became rare. If you have been plagued by what seems to be "spiritual warfare" on a regular basis, we suggest you spend time with the Lord and allow Him to remove emotional land mines.

How do we know if we have entered into enemy territory? Negative emotions. How do we know if we are in God's territory? The fruit of the Spirit, of course! God's emotions.

> *Emotions were created to be*
> *conduits of God's love.*

49

## NOTES

1.  M. Gershon, *The Second Brain,* (New York, NY; HarperCollins, 2003). Original work published 1999.

2.  There are millions of neurons in the enteric nervous systemas well as in the central nervous system (CNS) consisting of the brain, spinal cord, and peripheral nerves. Millions of neurons line the walls of our esophagus, intestines, stomach, and colon. The left vagus nerve connects the brain's emotional center with the gut. Neuropeptides, molecules of emotion, are released throughout the body and brain, transmitting emotional information to every cell, organ, and system of the entire body.

3.  Neuropeptides, molecules of emotion, are continuously released throughout our body and brain, transmitting emotional information to every cell, organ, and system. Our cells have receptors that "read" emotional information and react in a physiological response. For example, when we are embarrassed, we blush. Fear increases our heart rate. Sadness may cause us to cry.

4.  Our physical heart doesn't *transmit* emotional information. It only *receives* emotional information and responds accordingly. It only has approximately 40,000 neurons that regulate our heart beat. You could think of the central nervous system and enteric nervous systems as powerful *computers,* but the physical heart is more like a *computer chip.*

5.  Something from the outside must break into the feedback loop to change the dynamics within the system. Otherwise, the same cycle just keeps repeating itself.

    Each one of us has a feeling-thought feedback loop that connects our head, heart, organs, and systems. Because the brain automatically links our thoughts and emotions together, it's impossible to separate them. They are inextricably joined as feeling-thought units.

    One example of a feedback loop is when the pancreas increases the production of insulin after we eat. If blood sugar levels rise, the endocrine system triggers insulin production in the pancreas to counteract the increase and return blood sugar levels to normal. At this point, the pancreas is signaled to stop producing and releasing the insulin. It is a closed unit that operates automatically.

When we open the door of our heart in prayer, the love of God can flow into our whole being. God breaks into the loop and changes us. If the door of our heart is already open to the Lord, all we have to do to be forgiven is yield to His forgiveness.

6.    D. Vergano, "Emotions rule the brain's decisions," USA Today: Science and Space, August 6, 2006. Retrieved June 22, 2012 from http://usatoday30.usatoday.com/tech/science/discoveries/2006-08-06-brain-study_x.htm.

7.    Brother Lawrence, *The Practice of the Presence of God,* (Brewster, MA: Paraclete Press, 2010). Originally published as a brief booklet shortly after Lawrence's death in 1691.

*Chapter 4*

# OUR HIDING PLACE

The Bible uses many metaphors that describe God as the defender and protector of His people. He is our Rock, Fortress, High Tower, Hiding Place, Shield, and Dwelling Place. Psalm 91 is perhaps the most well-known hymn celebrating God as our Protector and Deliverer. *"He who dwells in the secret place of the Most High shall abide under the shadow of the Almighty. I will say of the Lord, 'He is my refuge and my fortress; my God, in Him I will trust'"* (Ps. 91:1-2).

Although we have little need for mountain fortresses to survive during an enemy siege today, in Old Testament days having a refuge to flee to from enemies was a very real need. Stronghold cities, high towers, and ramparts allowed residents of regions to escape and gain a strategic advantage when defending themselves from enemy forces. Rocks and caves provided personal safety for David during the 17 years he ran from Saul: *"David stayed in strongholds in the wilderness...Saul sought him every day, but God did not deliver him into his hand"* (1 Sam. 23:14).

*God is our refuge and strength, a very present help in trouble*
*(Psalm 46:1).*

We find our own place of safety when we "hide" in the presence of God. When we drop down to our spirit and stay in peace, God Himself guards us and delivers us from the enemy. The enemy can't touch us when we are kept by the power of God!

> ### *We are hidden in God.*

## PUT ON THE NEW MAN

Rather than running to a stronghold in the hills, God has established Himself a fortress in our own heart. When we drop down to our spirit, we enter His presence, our Hiding Place. God keeps us safe. God delivers us from the snare of the enemy.

Let's look more closely at the great deliverance the Lord has made available. When we get saved much is provided for us, but we are responsible for appropriating our inheritance and equipment. Therefore, when we are told to "put off" the old man and his deeds and "put on" the new man, we need to know how to do that (see Eph. 4:22-24). Of course, at the time of our salvation we *began* the process of putting off and putting on and were made a new creation in our spirit. However, we must continue the procedure in our daily walk.

Whether or not we are aware of it, we have enlisted in God's army. Every soldier must go to boot camp and be trained before entering into battle. Training includes wearing the right uniform, learning how to use weapons, and obeying the commander's orders. We have been issued spiritual clothing for warfare, but we are responsible for wearing it. Using the metaphor of soldiers engaging in warfare, we are told to:

- Put on the whole armor of God (Eph. 6:11).

- Put on the breastplate of righteousness (Eph. 6:14).

- Put on the armor of light (Rom. 13:12).

- Put on the Lord Jesus Christ (Rom. 13:14).

How do we do that? We drop down and become immersed in the presence of God. The Greek word for "put on" is *enduo,* which means "to sink into as being clothed." When we drop down to our spirit, we put off carnality and put on supernatural clothing. We can liken it to baptism in water. We sink into the water and it completely surrounds us. When we sink into Christ within, He surrounds us. He is both within us and around us.

*Enduo* is used in another Scripture verse that sheds even more light on the subject. Jesus told His disciples: *"Behold, I send the Promise of My Father upon you; but tarry in the city of Jerusalem until you are **endued** with power from on high"* (Luke 24:49). Only when we tap into the power of God in our heart can we obey the command to be *"strong in the Lord and in the power of His might"* (Eph. 6:10).

With God as our fortress, how can the enemy get to us? He can't. We only become vulnerable when we allow the enemy to cause us to lose our peace. The *"peace of God, which surpasses all understanding, will guard* [our] *hearts and minds through Christ Jesus"* (Phil. 4:7). No foe can get past God. We can make ourselves vulnerable, however, if we fail to guard our emotions, thoughts, and choices.

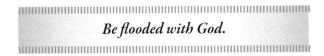

*Be flooded with God.*

## WILD EMOTIONS, THOUGHTS, AND CHOICES

Do you ever have some emotions, thoughts, or choices that "run wild"? As we use our spiritual tools in our everyday walk, we can corral those loose emotions, thoughts, and choices. When we give them to Christ within, He fits them into a structure of life that is shaped by

Him. We already possess the tools we need; they are within us and they will remove barriers or obstructions so that we can build our lives filled with supernatural peace.

How do we deal with toxic emotions? Forgiveness. Runaway thoughts? Present them to Christ within and let Him wash through our emotions until we feel peace. Choices? Release them into the hands of God until we feel peace. If we regularly find ourselves making the same bad choice over and over, we should drop down in prayer and ask the Lord to show us when the cycle began. Forgiveness will eradicate the root, freeing us to live life as God intended.

## THINKING GOD'S THOUGHTS

We receive revelation from God when our spirit is connected to Him. God reveals truth to our heart, and our heart informs our head. Truth is quickened in our heart and automatically rises up to our consciousness. We can't force information we know in our head down into our heart. Our logical reasoning can operate independently from God. As believers, we can allow the Lord to rule our thoughts or we can refuse His lordship and stay in control. Know, however, that anything we receive from God is far superior to our mental analysis. (Guarding our thought life is covered in greater detail in chapter six.)

> *For as the heavens are higher than the earth, so are my ways higher than your ways, and my thoughts than your thoughts* (Isaiah 55:9).

## CHOICES CREATE OUR FUTURE

Have you ever felt a check in your spirit? That was an inner *no* of the conscience. Have you ever had a Scripture or idea "quickened" to you? That was the inner *yes* as well. Our belly is the location of the will where we are able to make decisions and choices.

The belly or gut is not only the seat of our spirit and emotions but also the seat of our will and conscience—the faculties of choice and decision-making. A word commonly used for the will in the original Hebrew is *kidneys*, often translated "reins."

*The righteous God trieth the hearts and reins* (Psalm 7:9b KJV).

*I am He which searcheth the reins and hearts: and I will give unto every one of you according to your works* (Revelation 2:23 KJV).

How can we get the mind of the Lord when making choices? The presence or absence of the peace of God is an amazing key for receiving guidance from the Lord. When we are unsure about what direction to take, we must first become neutral about our options. In other words, we must first let go of our own opinions and allow God to reveal His choice. Our carnal preferences and dislikes can prevent us from hearing from the Lord clearly. The safest place to be is in the center of God's will (see Rom. 8:28).

*"For I know the plans I have for you," says the Lord. "They are plans for good and not for disaster, to give you a future and a hope"* (Jeremiah 29:11 NLT).

Suppose you have a decision to make about two possible choices. Get in an attitude of prayer and present each possibility before the Lord, one at a time. Peace indicates "yes" while an uncomfortable feeling in your gut means "no." Occasionally, we may not feel discomfort per se, but notice that the presence of God increases more on one option than the other. That is a "yes." If you get no clear increase of peace or "check" in your spirit, that usually means "wait." The timing may be wrong or God may have another option that has not been made known to you.

*Let the peace* (soul harmony which comes) *from Christ rule* (act as umpire continually) *in your hearts [deciding and settling with finality all questions that arise in your minds]* (Colossians 3:15 AMPC).

> ### *Choose God's choices.*

When we step out of the will of God, we become vulnerable and the enemy can influence the choices we make. The Lord has a good plan for our life, but the devil has an evil plan (see 1 Pet. 5:8). For a blessed life, choose God's choices.

> *You once walked according to the course of this world, according to the prince of the power of the air, the spirit who now works in the sons of disobedience, among whom also we all once conducted ourselves in the lusts of our flesh* (Ephesians 2:2-3).

## PEACE WITH GOD, SELF, AND OTHERS

When we first become a believer, we make our peace with God. We are reconciled to God. Paul said, *"Therefore, having been justified by faith, we have peace with God through our Lord Jesus Christ"* (Rom. 5:1). Not only do we open our heart to the Lord at salvation, we should continually keep the door of our heart open to Him and allow Him to rule.

As soon as we open the door of our heart to Him, we connect to Christ within. The *"fountain"* of living water that springs up in our heart gives us life (see John 4:14). After we are saved we have access to the river of peace all the time. To enjoy the peace of God in daily life, we simply drop our bucket down into the well. The goal is to learn to live with our "bucket" down all the time. Peace becomes a lifestyle.

*I will extend peace...like a river* (Isaiah 66:12).

**Peace grounds us.**

### Practice: Changing Focus

Think of a stressful situation. How does it feel in your gut? A little turmoil, chaos, or anxiety, perhaps? We all have different words that we use for this feeling. It doesn't feel peaceful when we picture a stressful or painful situation.

Now picture a pleasant memory such as a vacation. How does that feel? Good? Where did that bad feeling you were feeling before go? It didn't go away. It just went under the surface. It can come back as soon as it's triggered.

It is clear that we simply must take dealing with negative emotions seriously to stay in our Hiding Place, our place of sure deliverance.

*You are my hiding place; You shall preserve me from trouble;*
*You shall surround me with songs of deliverance* (Psalm 32:7).

*Chapter 5*

# EMOTIONS AND FORGIVENESS

## By Dr. Jen

In the time of Jesus, Jewish law specified that it was unnecessary to forgive someone more than three times, citing Amos 1:3–13. In this particular passage of Scripture, God forgave Israel's enemies three times, then punished them. Peter, wishing to appear especially benevolent, asked Jesus if he should forgive as many as seven times. Jesus replied by telling him he should forgive *"seventy times seven"* times (see Matt. 18:21-22). By this Jesus didn't mean to literally raise the numerical count from 3 to 490 (which is a number beyond counting for all practical purposes anyway). He was saying that we must forgive every time we are hurt or offended. We must forgive and keep on forgiving.

After Jesus answered Peter's question about forgiveness, He told a parable about the kingdom of heaven and forgiveness (see Matt. 18:23–35). A king forgave the debt of a servant who owed him an impossibly large sum of money. However, that same servant turned right around and choked a man who owed him a small amount then threw him into prison. When the king found out what his servant had done he became angry, threw the servant into prison, and turned him over to the tormentors.

Jesus died for us and forgave us a debt we couldn't pay. In light of His goodness, Jesus instructs *us* to be forgivers as well. God doesn't throw us into an actual prison when we are disobedient, but unforgiveness becomes a prison of our own making, opening us up to demonic torment. Additionally, when we have unforgiveness toward someone they have emotional control over us. We are trapped by our own failure to forgive. Only forgiveness sets us free.

Forgiveness should be a regular part of our life because the Holy Spirit is a forgiving Spirit. God wouldn't tell us to do something He hasn't given us the grace to accomplish. Grace is the personal presence of Christ living His life through us. What we can't do, Jesus can. Therefore, the Lord has given us the ability to forgive because Jesus forgives through us.

> *Be kind to one another, tenderhearted, forgiving one another, even as God in Christ forgave you* (Ephesians 4:32).

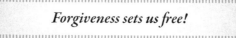

*Forgiveness sets us free!*

## A MATTER OF THE HEART

Forgiveness is not mental assent or saying the words, "I forgive." Forgiveness is a matter of the heart and must include the emotions. The antidote for all toxic emotions is forgiveness. It washes out the poison and replaces it with supernatural peace.

One of the most important lessons as followers of Jesus is to learn is how to yield our will to God. When we yield our will to God's will, God works in us and through us. We rest in Him and He works in us.

*It is God who is at work in you, both to will and to work for His good pleasure* (Philippians 2:13 NASB).

*For he who has entered His rest has himself also ceased from his works as God did from His* (Hebrews 4:10).

---

### When we rest, God works.

---

## Practice

Close your eyes and **pray.** Place your hand on your belly to remind you to focus on Christ in you. When you change your focus from the thoughts in your head to Christ within, that awareness automatically means you have made a spirit-to-Spirit connection with God.

Yield, or relax, even more. Peace feels gentle and subtle most of the time, so don't expect lightning bolts. You are touching the presence of the Lord.

Now, think of something you are grateful to God for doing in your life. A feeling of joy usually accompanies gratitude. That is the fruit of the Spirit.

NOTE: The next time you are in a worship service and sense the anointing in the room, it didn't fall out of heaven. It is the product of love toward God released from the hearts of those worshiping.

## DISTANCE IS A DECEPTION

As mentioned previously, distance is a deception. Christ *in us* is our *"hope of glory"* (Col. 1:27). At the time of salvation, we opened our heart and welcomed Him in. After salvation we touch His presence every time we open our heart and include Him in our life. Unfortunately, many believers live in their heads more than their hearts, thinking of Christ in heaven instead of at hand (see Matt. 4:17).

In John 15:5, Jesus tells us to "abide" in Him. We abide by opening the door of our heart, yielding to Christ within, and keeping the connection open. We know we are abiding when we feel the peace of His presence. Jesus is the Prince of Peace. When Jesus rules our life, His peace manifests. As soon as we drop down and yield we feel the peace of His presence.

> *When Jesus rules, peace manifests.*

The same Prince of Peace who took authority over a storm on the Sea of Galilee also has authority over the storms in our life. As Romans 16:20 assures us, *The God of peace will crush Satan under your feet.* Peace is living in the presence of the Prince of Peace for *"He Himself is our peace"* (Eph. 2:14).

Forgiveness is not releasing someone from responsibility, being a doormat, or forgetting. Forgiveness is not unconditionally reconciling with a person while failing to establish appropriate boundaries. We are commanded to forgive a thief, but we don't have to give him a key to our front door.

> *Apply forgiveness whenever*
> *peace is lost.*

## CHRIST THE FORGIVER

Christ the forgiver Himself forgives through us so we don't "try" to forgive. Christ forgives through us and loves through us. We allow Christ the forgiver within to do all the work. We simply yield our will and allow Christ to forgive.

Forgiveness must include the mind, will, and *emotions*. Our mind remembers, our will opens the door of our heart so Jesus can work, and our emotions are conduits allowing forgiveness to flow. Until the emotions have been impacted, forgiveness is incomplete. Forgiveness washes out negative emotions and gets us back to the place of peace. It is just as instant as it was when we got saved. When you were saved, how long did it take for you to receive forgiveness? It didn't take days or hours. You opened your heart and forgiveness was instantly yours. Why should forgiveness be any different after we have Christ the forgiver in our heart? Was it easy for Him then, but now it's hard? Of course not.

> *Yield and let Christ*
> *forgive through you.*

## WHO TO FORGIVE

Forgiveness goes in three directions—toward God, self, and others. Sometimes we need to forgive in two or even three directions. If in doubt, forgive. You can't love or forgive too much!

### God

God didn't do anything wrong, but people get angry at Him anyway. Sometimes individuals feel hurt that God didn't do what they wanted Him to do or become angry that God didn't prevent something from happening. Forgiving God gets our heart right by releasing our judgments against Him.

### Self

If we are angry, disappointed, or ashamed of ourselves, we need to receive forgiveness for judging ourselves so harshly. Frequently, people are much harder on themselves than others!

*Others*

Release forgiveness to other people. It sets you free!

## HOW TO FORGIVE

The steps of forgiveness are not a "method" we came up with. They are a description of how I (Dennis) observed the Holy Spirit working in my own life and in the lives of thousands of others with whom I have prayed. Jen and I consider ourselves to be facilitators who simply follow what the Holy Spirit is doing. It is all about pointing believers to Christ within so He can work. A few years after we began developing teaching materials, Jen asked the Lord to show her a simpler way to teach others. He gave her the words "first, feel, forgive." It is less difficult to remember three words than half a page of explanation. This has proven to be much easier for individuals to recall.

We have a three by five blue card available called, appropriately enough, the "Blue Card" that briefly lists the three basic steps of forgiveness, as well as how to dismantle mental strongholds and fill emotional needs.

*Close your eyes and pray.* You may want to place your hand on your belly to remind you to be aware of Christ within. We are asking the Lord to bring to our mind anything that needs healing in our heart. Practice forgiving by following the steps on the Blue Card which are listed below.

### Practice: Forgiveness

**Pray.** Close your eyes and focus on Christ within in an attitude of prayer.

**First.** What is the first person or situation that comes to mind—an image or memory?

**Feel.** Feel the feeling. Allow yourself to **feel**. What emotion do you feel in your gut when you picture that person or situation? (Every thought has a corresponding emotion.)

**Forgive.** Yield to Christ the forgiver within and allow a river of forgiveness to flow from the belly until the emotion changes to peace. If you are forgiving yourself, receive forgiveness from Christ in you. If you are upset with another person, allow forgiveness to flow out to them. If you are angry at or disappointed with God, forgive Him.

In most cases, we only need the three steps of *First-Feel-Forgive*. (Occasionally, additional steps may be needed to complete the work. These additional steps are explained in later chapters.) Only what God says is reality or fact. Historical evidence is not necessarily reality. When we forgive and get peace, deliverance is usually automatic.

Always deal with the emotion first. Negative emotions give ground to the enemy. When Jesus replaces an unpleasant emotion with the supernatural fruit of the Spirit, we have spiritual power to resist evil spirits. We cannot skip dealing with our emotions because any negative emotion gives demonic activity permission to oppress us.

> *Negative emotions give*
> *the enemy ground.*

## TOXIC EMOTIONS ATTRACT EVIL

Demonic hitchhikers can gain permission to torment us and influence our life via negative emotions even when we can't sense the presence of evil. Working as a school psychologist, I traveled to several different schools in the county of my employment. I had noticed in the past that every once in a while a strong-willed teacher would clash with me and cause a great deal of trouble.

The first year Dennis and I were married, I began working at a new school and one teacher seemed antagonistic toward me. Suddenly, with my eyes wide open I saw in the spirit a bevy of translucent bats swarm all around her and then attach all over her! I thought, "Oh, no! It's happening again!"

When I drove home that afternoon, I ran to Dennis and told him what had happened. We sat down to pray and he told me to focus on the first person or situation that came to mind. I instantly pictured a former teacher of mine from childhood. Suffice it to say I had a difficult year with her.

Feeling the hurt and frustration in my gut, I let a river of forgiveness flow out to her from my heart. Instantly, the toxic emotions left and were replaced with supernatural peace. The next day I returned to work, and the seemingly antagonistic teacher was pleasant and calm and never caused me a problem again. The lesson I learned from this was to deal with *every* negative emotion quickly because I believe they *all* attract evil spirits to work harm in our life.

> *Deal with every negative
> emotion quickly!*

## GENERATIONAL SIN

A familiar spirit is a demon assigned to an individual. A practitioner of the occult may welcome psychic information and/or power from a demonic source.

> *Turn not to those [mediums] who have familiar spirits or to wizards; do not seek them out to be defiled by them. I am the Lord your God* (Leviticus 19:31 AMPC).

> *The person who turns to those who have familiar spirits and to wizards, [being unfaithful to Israel's Maker Who is her Husband, and thus] playing the harlot after them, I will set My face against that person and will cut him off from among his people [that he may not be included in the atonement made for them]* (Leviticus 20:6 AMPC).

In the Book of Acts, Paul and Silas were in Philippi and encountered a slave girl with a familiar spirit, a spirit of divination.

> *Now it happened, as we went to prayer, that a certain slave girl possessed with a spirit of divination met us, who brought her masters much profit by fortune-telling. This girl followed Paul and us, and cried out, saying, "These men are the servants of the Most High God, who proclaim to us the way of salvation." And this she did for many days. But Paul, greatly annoyed, turned and said to the spirit, "I command you in the name of Jesus Christ to come out of her." And he came out that very hour* (Acts 16:16–18).

Both generational curses and blessings pass down family lines (see Exod. 34:7; Deut. 7:9). *Familiar spirits* assigned to a family hitchhike on sinful behavior and perpetuate it through several generations as a generational curse. For a generational sin to begin operating in an individual's life, it must have a specific "entry point" before it takes effect in an individual's life.

If you believe that some type of generational sin is operating in your life, ask God. You don't have to try to figure it out on your own. The Lord will be faithful to show you where it got started in your life. Pray according to the guidelines in the next practice section.

When Dennis and I were married, he began praying me through issues and teaching me how to go to Christ within for healing. A situation with my mother came to mind. Dennis and I both felt a demonic hitchhiker manifest, and he said, "Your face just changed. I saw in a flash your mother's face superimposed over yours." That visual impression came from a familiar spirit passed down through my family line.[1] Dennis instructed me to let forgiveness flow to my mother and to let it continue to flow back through my family line. Instantly the evil presence lifted and I felt peace. In that case, a generational sin came to the forefront in the process of praying through a cycle of issues.[2]

## Practice: Self-Deliverance

**Pray.** If you are concerned about whether you need deliverance, close your eyes and **pray.** If you feel peace and no particular area comes to mind, that's good. We are to let the peace of God rule in our life. If a particular person or situation does stand out, feel the feeling in your gut. Start with forgiveness until you get peace.

**First.** If you have opened a door to torment by sinning, picture the sin.

**Feel.** Feel the negative emotion in your gut.

**Forgive.** Forgive and/or receive forgiveness until it changes to peace. (If another person is involved, forgive them, too.) Now, yield and receive repentance as a gift.

Yield to the Deliverer. If you still feel external pressure or oppression after you have peace in your heart, yield to Christ the deliverer in you, and welcome Him to rise up within you and push off any religious hitchhiker. Continue to yield to Him until you feel the pressure in the atmosphere lift.

Once the oppression lifts, stay in the peace of God. The enemy can't touch the fruit of the Spirit. If you accidently lose your peace, receive forgiveness and you will feel peace again.

## Practice: Familiar Spirits and Generational Sin

If you are concerned about a particular sin that runs in your family line and believe you may have given in to it or are concerned about prior involvement in the occult allow the Lord to cleanse you and set you free.

**Pray.** Close your eyes and get in an attitude of prayer.

**First.** Ask the Lord to show you the entry point—the first person or situation that comes to mind.

**Feel.** When you see a person or situation, momentarily feel the attached emotion.

**Forgive.** Receive forgiveness for taking in something God didn't give you. Allow a river of forgiveness to flow from Christ within to the person or release the situation into God's hands.

Family. For generational sin, release forgiveness back through your family line to ancestors who opened up to that spirit.

## NOTES

1.  A familiar spirit is a spirit assigned to an individual due to occult activity or one that   is passed down a family line creating "pressure" to engage in a particular sin as a generational influence. Generational sin becomes operative at a particular time in the life of an individual when they engage in the sin. Individuals involved in the occult often invite the presence of evil spirits to partner with them. The spirits of dead humans don't "stay behind" on earth. Spirits return to God (see Eccles. 12:7). However, demons can mimic a person who has died and deceive an individual by pretending to be someone who has passed on. *"Give no regard to mediums and familiar spirits; do not seek after them, to be defiled by them: I am the Lord your God"* (Lev. 19:31). And: *"And when they say to you, 'Seek those who are mediums and wizards, who whisper and mutter,' should not a people seek their God? Should they seek the dead on behalf of the living?"* (Isa. 8:19).

2.  When we pray through several issues in one prayer session rather than just one, we call it a "cycle of issues." A single prayer session should generally not cover more than three to five emotional healings because it can become emotionally exhausting to deal with multiple negative emotions, particularly when they have been suppressed a long time.

# SECTION TWO

# WINNING THE WAR

*Chapter 6*

# PESKY THOUGHTS

We shouldn't accept something just because we hear it in our head. There is an old saying about thoughts that is actually quite true: "You can't stop a bird from flying over your head, but you don't have to let it make a nest in your hair." The Bible instructs us to *take captive every thought to make it obedient to Christ*" (2 Cor. 10:5 NIV).

## TAKING THOUGHTS CAPTIVE

How do we take thoughts captive and make them obedient to Christ in a practical way? We must begin by making two distinctions. First, we must start from our true identity so we can stand in our authority in Christ. Second, we must differentiate between inside and outside to know whether we are dealing with flesh or evil spirit.

### 1. Make a distinction: "That's not me."

Start from the place of the new creation you, fused together with Christ. Make a distinction between the new creation and the thoughts and impressions that the world, flesh, or the devil want to impose on you. The new creation loves God and loves His Word. The new creation always agrees with God. Anything that does not line up with the nature and character of God in you originates from either your flesh or demonic hitchhikers, not the real you!

Our true identity is the person God created us to be—a new creation in Christ. Paul said, *"Therefore, if anyone is in Christ, he is a new creation; old things have passed away; behold, all things have become new"* (2 Cor. 5:17). A born-again believer is more than a conqueror (see Rom. 8:37). We must start from that place of victory. If we hear a thought that doesn't sound like the new creation, we shouldn't accept it. It doesn't matter if a negative thought comes from us or the devil. If it isn't something God would say, don't receive it.

> *The new creation always*
> *agrees with God.*

An emotionally expressive young woman named Renee started attending our church. It wouldn't be an exaggeration to say we have never known anyone else who made an altar call quite as exciting as she did on her first visit. Later, she told us that she had been asked to leave churches in the past because of her hysterical behavior.

First we told her that it wasn't necessary to give emotions the fullest expression possible, although it is necessary to feel the emotion somewhat in order to present it to Christ within. Renee calmed down for a moment. Then she started sobbing again and said, "I am hearing in my head that if I start coming to this church I will destroy it." We assured her that thought was not coming from God.

Next, we told Renee to renounce that thought and gave her some "homework" for the coming week. We said, "During the coming week, whenever you hear a thought that doesn't sound like something God would say—we don't care if you are saying it or the devil is saying it—renounce the thought instead of owning it." We told her to identify with the new creation and say, "That's not me!" By the very next week she was remarkably changed and made rapid progress both spiritually and emotionally from that time on.

### *Know when "that's not me!"*

## 2. Make a distinction: Inside or outside

The second distinction we must make is to differentiate between flesh and demonic influence. Unless we discern what needs to be sanctified and what requires deliverance, we will struggle with confusion. It is vital to know the *source* of what afflicts us—flesh or spirit. We can't cast out flesh and we can't sanctify a demon. Once we understand the source, we can yield to Christ within to heal emotional wounds through sanctification and be delivered from demonic oppression through the authority we as believers have in Christ.

*Check inside.* When we feel oppression, we should first check *inside*, in our gut. We feel our emotions *inside* us. We recognize demonic involvement by what we feel *outside* us. When we feel a negative emotion inside, we should always deal with our emotions first through forgiveness. Pray "first, feel, forgive." We can't resist unless we first have peace. Peace is the place of power.

*Check outside.* When we have peace but perceive *outside* oppression, the pressure is external. As soon as we have peace, we are submitting (yielding) to God. Now we have the spiritual authority and strength to resist. We submit to God, resist the devil, and he has to flee. We already have victory when we are in the place of peace.

> *Therefore submit to God. Resist the devil and he will flee from you* (James 4:7).

Yield or *submit* to Christ within, stay in peace, and *resist* external oppression. "I hear you knocking but you can't come in!" Supernatural peace will guard our heart and our mind (see Phil. 4:7). Don't be surprised if the outside oppression doesn't lift immediately, although it usually does. It has to go sooner or later. When we stay in peace and refuse to give in to anything negative in the atmosphere, we build spiritual strength. Whether it goes instantly or lingers for a while, we win.

> *Peace is the place of power.*

The first year Dennis and I (Jen) were married, I had many fear issues, which we dealt with one by one. Fear often manifested both as an emotion I felt in my gut and a pressure I sensed outside in the room. Every time I felt fear of any kind, I asked God, "Where did that come from?" The Lord showed me situations in my past where I had given in to fear. He often pointed out circumstances or people causing me to worry. I dealt with every fear through forgiveness until I felt peace.

After gaining much victory over fear, I was tested. Several times I awakened during the night feeling fear in the bedroom. First I checked inside me to see if I felt peace. When I knew I was at peace, I yielded even more to Christ within and ignored the fear in the atmosphere around me. In so doing, I successfully resisted the oppression and didn't give in. The presence of God increased, the fearful atmosphere dissipated, and I fell back to sleep.

## TWO CATEGORIES OF THOUGHTS

### Simple Distractions

When we lose our peace due to a mild distraction or fleeting worry, we should renounce it (silently or aloud) and release it to Christ within until we feel peace again. Our focus is on Him instead of the intrusive thought (see 2 Cor. 10:5). We give power to what we give attention to.

> *We give power to what we*
> *give attention to.*

### Mental Strongholds

Most of the time, emotional wounds do not have a lie, or mental stronghold, attached to them. However, when a lie is believed it blocks the truth from being received. Truth bounces off the stronghold like water off a stone.

A person might say, "I know the Bible says God loves me, but...." That word *but* is a sure indication that a mental stronghold is preventing them from receiving the truth. To demolish a mental stronghold we must start by dealing with the emotion fortifying it. Lies come in at the time of emotional wounding. The presence of a negative emotion gives the lie power. Forgiveness replaces the pain with supernatural peace. When we have peace, we have authority to dislodge the lie. Then truth can rise up from our spirit and be written on our heart.

An individual may come to believe a lie is their "identity" if they have lived with it over a long time. They may also be able to point at historical "evidence" that has fortified the lie. If someone hears the thought "I am a failure," they may argue that it's true because they can remember specific instances of failure in their life. Behavior does not determine identity. Past performance is what we have *done*, not who we *are*. We may *fail* from time to time, but that doesn't make *failure* our identity.

Here are some examples of mental strongholds:

- "I am unworthy." What does God say?

- "I can't do anything right." What does God say?

- "I never belong." What does God say?

- "I am a hopeless mess." What does God say?

- "I have to be in control." What does God say?

## TESTING THOUGHTS

There are three tests we should apply to our thought life. First, test the thought by the spirit behind it. When God speaks to us, *His* Spirit is on the words. If the thought has any other nature on it, don't receive it. A word from God, even a corrective word, has all the love of heaven behind it. Can you feel the love of God on the thought? If the thought feels condemning, accusatory, or intrusive it is not God.

> *God's nature is on His words*
> *and produces good fruit.*

Second, test the thought by the words. Does the thought agree with the Bible? God never disagrees with His written Word. Does it sound like something God would say? It doesn't matter if you are saying it or the enemy is saying it; if it's not God don't accept it.

Finally, test the thought by the fruit. Does it feel like the fruit of the Spirit? God corrects us to get us back on course with Him, not to make us feel condemned. If we acted on the thought, what fruit would it produce? Everything that comes from God produces good fruit.

## PULLING DOWN STRONGHOLDS

All thoughts have two lines of communication—the *words* of the thought and the *authority*, or power, connected to it. The *emotion* connected to the thought is what gives it authority. We can't stop hearing voices, but we can resist successfully if the voice has no authority behind it.

We can hear the voice of God, but we can hear other voices as well—the world, the past, the flesh, and the devil. We can't silence all the different voices, but we can break their power in our life. In other words, forgiveness removes the power but not the line of communication. Even though we may still hear a voice, when it has no authority, or power, we can easily ignore it. We can't stop the communication, but forgiveness removes its power to torment us.

> *We can't stop a thought, but we can break its power over us.*

If I heard a thought such as, "You are a bad ice skater," but I am not emotionally invested in ice skating, that thought has no power. However, if I heard a voice saying, "You're a failure," and I had been wounded by those same words once spoken by my father, the pain would be triggered every time I had the thought. To defuse the thought and nullify its authority, I must forgive my father to replace the pain with peace. If I heard that thought again, I would simply drop down to my spirit and feel peace in my heart. I could then successfully resist that voice by ignoring it. Again, *"Submit to God. Resist the devil and he will flee"* (James 4:7).

To pull down a mental stronghold, always begin by dealing with the emotion through forgiveness. When we don't have peace, we don't have spiritual authority. When a negative emotion is present, we are operating out of the wrong kingdom. When we have peace, we are in the place of supernatural power that can defeat any lie. Most emotional wounds do not have lies attached, although a lie does come in at the time of emotional wounding. A lie is believed in only one out of every 30 or 40 instances.

Usually the initial three steps of first-feel-forgive are sufficient. However, pulling down a mental stronghold requires an additional step after we forgive and get peace. We must next renounce the lie and allow the Lord to replace it with the truth. To *first-feel-forgive,* we add the step "fact." No matter what we previously believed as a falsehood, God and His Word are scriptural fact.

*Peace is the place of power.*

## Practice: Start with Forgiveness

**First.** What is the first person or situation that comes to mind—an image or memory?

**Feel.** Feel the feeling. Allow yourself to **feel**. What emotion do you feel in your gut when you picture that person or situation? (Every thought has a corresponding emotion.)

**Forgive.** Yield to Christ the forgiver within and allow a river of forgiveness to flow from the belly until the emotion changes to peace. If you are forgiving yourself, receive forgiveness from Christ in you. Allow forgiveness to flow out to others. If you are angry at or disappointed with God, forgive Him. If you are upset with yourself, yield and receive forgiveness from Christ within.

## Practice: Remove the Mental Stronghold

Fact. After forgiving and getting peace, if there is a lie, renounce it out loud. Next, ask the Lord for the truth (scriptural fact) and receive it. (Lies always come in at the time of emotional wounding. When we forgive and get peace, we are in the place of power with the spiritual authority to dislodge the lie.)

*Chapter 7*

# INSTANT FAITH DETOX

## BY DR. JEN

Prior to meeting Dennis and learning the secrets for forgiveness, I was very angry at someone who had hurt me. For two years I begged God to help me forgive, but the pain and anger continued to surface each time that person came to mind. As a result, discouragement took over and my prayers ceased. Based on my experience, I fabricated a false theology that forgiveness is hard and takes a long time. My faith shut down and I gave up.

For believers, our spirit is a new creation that always believes God and His Word. However, our spirit, soul, and body are a unit. Each part of us affects the other parts. When our soul gets wounded, disappointed, or discouraged it can quench our spirit, create barriers in our relationship with God, and cause our heart to "shut the door" on faith. When we stop believing God will hear us we can give up on Him.

*Hope deferred makes the heart sick, but when the desire comes, it is a tree of life* (Proverbs 13:12).

## DETOX YOUR SPIRIT

What is your experience? Have you been disappointed that you didn't get answers to some prayers? Have you been plagued by discouragement and doubt? Many believers have their faith quenched by enduring a chronic illness or experiencing "faith catastrophes" with friends or loved ones. We may continue to pray with a measure of "hope so" that really isn't faith at all. When we lower our expectations and doubt that God will really work on our behalf, our relationship with Him suffers. God doesn't become distant, but discouraged believers often distance themselves from Him.

## SIX STEPS OF DEFEAT

Our faith is sabotaged and our spirit quenched when we climb down the six steps of defeat. Remember, *six* is the number of flesh. We may:

1. Continue to pray with diminished faith

2. Lower our expectations

3. Change our theology

4. Give in to fear, doubt, and unbelief

5. Become bitter or depressed

6. Harden our heart

A change in theology may manifest as a toxic thought:

- "It's God's will for me to be sick and suffer; this is my cross to bear."

- "God is punishing me."

- "God only heals a few people, so I must not be one of the lucky ones."

- "The dispensation for healing has passed. It's not for today."

- "I'm unworthy."

- "I didn't pray/fast/try hard enough."

Toxic wounds and willpower walls are shackles forged by the soul. The soul can create "chains of bondage" that lock down our heart and quench our faith. However, Jesus says He came to *heal the bro-kenhearted*" and *"proclaim liberty to the captives"* (Luke 4:18). Only by removing the soulish chains can our faith be liberated. When we believe lies, truth cannot be received until the stronghold is cast down. However, Jesus can remove walls and toxic thoughts as easily as He cleanses and heals emotional pain through forgiveness.

> *For the word of God is living and powerful, and sharper than any two-edged sword, piercing even to the **division of soul and spirit**, and of joints and marrow, and is a discerner of the thoughts and intents of the heart. And there is no crea-ture hidden from His sight, but all things are naked and open to the eyes of Him to whom we must give account* (Hebrews 4:12-13).

## DROP DOWN

Everything changed for me when I met Dennis. He taught me how to drop down to my spirit and let the Forgiver in my own heart for-give *through* me. Jesus's forgiveness not only removed toxins, it broke through the walls in my heart. When I allowed Him to do the work, it was just as fast and effective as when I got saved. This is the how-to that transformed my whole life!

When I yielded my heart to Jesus in me, He took my pain, exchanged it for His peace, and restored my faith. Jesus hadn't made forgiveness hard—I had! Jesus didn't give up on me. I had quenched my spirit by shutting the door of my heart.

In addition, I had believed the false notion that Christianity is hard. That is so wrong! When I understood and applied the how-tos we're teaching you, I discovered the "simplicity of Christ" (see 2 Cor. 11:3). Everything is easy for Jesus! Our part is to *rest* in Him and *yield* to Him. Jesus said to the Pharisees:

> *"Which is easier, to say to the paralytic, 'Your sins are forgiven you,' or to say, 'Arise, take up your bed and walk'? But that you may know that the Son of Man has power on earth to forgive sins"—He said to the paralytic, "I say to you, arise, take up your bed, and go"* (Mark 2:9–11).

---

*Everything is easy for Jesus.*

---

Consider the parable of the True Vine in the Gospel of John, chapter 15. The Vine is always there but the branches can disconnect. The secret for living an abiding life is keeping our heart open and communing with the Lord. When our heart is open to Christ within, we abide in the Vine. We don't have to guess because when we sense the peace of God's presence we know our heart is open to Him.

> *I am the vine, you are the branches. He who abides in Me, and I in him, bears much fruit; for without Me you can do nothing* (John 15:5).

## OPEN, OPEN, OPEN

Our heart can be closed off due to ignorance, willpower walls, fear, doubt, and unbelief. Because we erect our own walls, we must *choose* to allow Jesus to remove them. To wash out toxic emotions in our soul, we must present them to Jesus in prayer. The solution for both walls and toxins is forgiveness.

> *Jesus removes our walls and*
> *toxins by forgiveness.*

A group of pastors and I (Dennis) went to Mexico on a mission trip many years ago, and while there we were asked to minister to a Anita, a young woman with severe agoraphobia. Agoraphobia is an anxiety disorder in which the sufferer fears and avoids places or situations that might induce panic and make them feel trapped, helpless, or embarrassed.

Anita was raised in Christian family but had become a prostitute. When she became pregnant she moved back home but hid in one room and refused to leave or let anyone else enter the room. After she gave birth, she continued to be reclusive and let no one in to check on the baby. The family, afraid the baby was not receiving proper care, reached out for pastoral help.

When we arrived we were able to convince her to let someone in the room. Anita was so demonized that her eyes were as black as coal and devoid of luster. As it turned out, she was very ashamed of her way of life and afraid of being judged, so she had hidden herself away from the world. As she received forgiveness, her emotional pain turned to peace and a spirit of shame lifted. Instantly her eyes became clear, her face glowed, and Anita handed the baby to her mother.

Deliverance had been instant, but full restoration can take some time. While we were still in Mexico, we got word that Anita left the room and joined her family in the rest of the house. After we returned to the states, we found out she was soon able to leave the house. A few months later Anita returned to church. Her world had become smaller and smaller. When she was healed, it got bigger and bigger.

God does not want us to live a confined, restricted life! Jesus tells us, *"The thief comes only in order to steal and kill and destroy. I came that they may have and enjoy life, and have it in abundance (to the full, till it overflows)"* (John 10:10 AMPC). When we close our heart, our world constricts. As we remove the walls through forgiveness and deliverance, we can be open to one another, open to God, and open to life! Life with a capital "L"!

## THREE STEPS TO RESTORED FAITH

When the Lord taught me (Dennis) about the fruit of the spirit of patience, I learned it as biblical hope or "holding the heart open until God comes through." Because God is love and love never fails, God always come through on our behalf when we trust Him (see 1 Cor. 13:8). Of course we must release how and when completely into God's hands. Hope is staying open until we receive the answer. While we wait, we remain in a place of prayerful anticipation, staying in communion with Father God. After removing walls, fear, doubt, unbelief, and mental strongholds, we are ready for our faith to be restored and be *"strengthened with might"* by the Holy Spirit in our inner man (Eph. 3:16).

> *He commanded them not to depart from Jerusalem, but to **wait** for the Promise of the Father* (Acts 1:4).

> *Hope is staying open until we receive the answer.*

1. **Love never fails.** Rest in the fact that God's love never fails. After releasing the situation into God's hands until you are at peace, wait for Love to come through.

*And now abide faith, hope, love, these three; but the greatest of these is love* (1 Corinthians 13:13).
*Love never fails* (1 Corinthians 13:8).

2. **Hope is open.** Wait in patience and stay open to God.
   *Hope deferred makes the heart sick, but when the desire comes, it is a tree of **life*** (Proverbs 13:12).

   - *Wait.* Stay in a place of prayerful expectation.

   - *Commune.* Spend time in prayer.

3. **Faith is inner assurance.** Faith is not "nothing." It is *substance*, the nature of God in us, confirming that God is true and His promises to us are reliable. When we were saved by faith, believing the gospel in our heart, we had an internal assurance that our faith in God for salvation was a real experience. It wasn't mere mental assent; a spiritual transaction had occurred. We can say with confidence "I know that I know," meaning both our *head* and *heart* bear witness. The most powerful faith builder is hearing from God. With inner barriers removed, we can hear much more clearly.

   *Faith is the **substance** of things hoped for, the evidence of things not seen* (Hebrews 11:1).

## Practice: Remove Barriers that Quench Your Spirit

### Remove Walls

**Pray.** Close your eyes and get in an attitude of prayer.

**First.** What is the first person or situation that comes to mind?

**Feel.** Feel the feeling. Allow yourself to **feel**. What emotion do you feel in your gut when you picture that person or situation? (Every thought has a corresponding emotion.)

**Forgive.** Yield to Christ the forgiver within and allow a river of forgiveness to flow from the belly until the emotion changes to peace. Allow forgiveness to flow out to others if you blame others. If you are angry at or disappointed with God, receive forgiveness for judging Him. If you are upset with yourself, yield and receive forgiveness from Christ within.

## Remove Fear, Doubt, and Unbelief

**Pray.** Close your eyes and get in an attitude of prayer.

**First.** What is the first person or situation that comes to mind. Where did fear, doubt, or unbelief get a foothold in your life?

**Feel.** Allow yourself to feel the toxic emotion(s) attached.

**Forgive.** Yield to Jesus the forgiver and receive forgiveness for allowing fear, doubt, and unbelief to have a place in your heart. Forgiveness washes out the poison and replaces it with supernatural peace. Allow forgiveness to flow out to others if you blame others. If you are angry at or disappointed with God, receive forgiveness for judging Him. If you are upset with yourself, yield and receive forgiveness from Christ within.

## Remove Mental Strongholds

To deal with a mental stronghold, always start with the emotion first through forgiveness until you feel peace. When we have peace, we are in the place of supernatural power that can defeat any lie. Most emotional wounds don't have lies attached. If there is a lie, it comes in at the time of emotional wounding. A lie is believed in one out of every 30 or 40 wounds. Usually the initial three steps of first-feel-forgive are sufficient for emotional healing.

## Start with Forgiveness

**Pray.** Close your eyes and get in an attitude of prayer.

**First.** What is the first person or situation that comes to mind?

**Feel.** Feel the feeling. Allow yourself to **feel.** What emotion you feel in your gut when you picture that person or situation? (Every thought has a corresponding emotion.)

**Forgive.** Yield to Christ the forgiver within and allow a river of forgiveness to flow from the belly until the emotion changes to peace. Allow forgiveness to flow out to others if you blame others. If you are angry at or disappointed with God, receive forgiveness for judging Him. If you are upset with yourself, yield and receive forgiveness from Christ within.

When you have peace, you are in the place of authority with power to dislodge the stronghold. Therefore, the next step is renouncing the lie aloud and allowing the Lord to replace it with the truth.

## Replace the Mental Stronghold with the Truth

Fact. Always deal with the emotion first to replace a negative emotion with peace. When we forgive and get peace, we are in the place of power with the spiritual authority to dislodge the lie. After forgiving and getting peace, renounce the lie out loud if there is one. Next, ask the Lord for the truth (scriptural fact) and receive it.

NOTE: Lies always come in at the time of emotional wounding, but very few emotional wounds have lies attached. In our experience, in only one out of every 30 or 40 wounds was a lie believed.

*Chapter 8*

# FIVE FUNCTIONS OF THE HUMAN SPIRIT

It is essential that we to know what our God-tools are and how to apply them. In addition, we must be trained in the functions of our human spirit.[1] Jesus tells us, *"He that believeth on me, as the scripture hath said, out of his belly shall flow rivers of living water"* (John 7:38 KJV). When we practice the five functions of our human spirit, we open our heart and let rivers of living water flow. We don't try; we simply open our heart and let God work through us. *"It is God who works in you both to **will** and to **do** for His good pleasure"* (Phil. 2:13).

What are some of our God-tools (see 2 Cor. 10:3–6)?

- Forgiveness (Acts 13:38; 1 John 1:9)

- Five functions of the human spirit (receiving, forgiving, loving, releasing, and resisting)

- Fruit of the Spirit (1 Cor. 13; Gal. 5:22-23)

- The armor of God (Eph. 6:10–18)

- Prayer (Matt. 6:9–13; Eph. 6:18)

- Fasting (Matt. 6: 16–18; Matt. 17:21)

- The Bible (Matt. 4:1–4; Eph. 6:17)

- Believer's authority in Christ (Luke 9:1, 10:19; James 4:7)

- The name of Jesus (Matt. 18:20; Mark 16:17)

- The Holy Spirit (John 14:26; John 7:38-39)

- The blood of Jesus (Rev. 12:11)

- The work of the Cross (1 Cor. 1:18; 2 Cor. 4:11-12)

- Spiritual gifts (Rom. 12:3–8; 1 Cor. 12:1–28; Eph. 4:7–16)

- Spiritual discernment (Phil. 1:9; Heb. 5:14)

- Patterns and principles of God (explained in Christian literature and teachings, salvation tracts, the Blue Card (see Chapter 5), and so forth)

However, it is important to remember that we can't apply the God-tools in the flesh. Only the Spirit gives life. Jesus says, *"Abide in Me, and I in you. As the branch cannot bear fruit of itself, unless it abides in the vine, neither can you, unless you abide in Me. I am the vine, you are the branches. He who abides in Me, and I in him, bears much fruit; for **without Me you can do nothing**"* (John 15:4-5).

The first loving function of the human spirit the Lord taught me (Dennis) was receiving. If you're reading this and saying, "I've never done this kind of thing before," we want you to stop trying and simply open your heart to experience and receive all God has for you. Opening the heart and yielding to the presence of Christ within is the way we get filled with more of God.

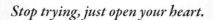

*Stop trying, just open your heart.*

## 1. RECEIVING

Receiving is your God-tool for spiritual nourishment and accepting impartation. Receiving is absorbing, drinking in, taking into your spirit. When you receive an increased measure of anointing, you can then pour out on behalf of others. You can only receive what you are open to, you can only give what you have received.

When we read scriptures like 1 John 3:1—*"Behold what manner of love the Father has bestowed on us, that we should be called children of God! Therefore the world does not know us, because it did not know Him"*—how do we receive that scripture? Do we think about it or memorize it, or should something deeper be experienced? We "drink it in" and welcome it into our heart.

*Drink, don't think.*

| Practice |
|---|
| Prayer. In an attitude of prayer, focus on the first Scripture verse that comes to mind and stay there for a while.<br>Receive. Receive it into your heart by welcoming it and drinking it in. |

## 2. FORGIVING

The second function of the human spirit is forgiveness. Forgiveness provides cleansing for our heart and sets us free from negative emotions. Anytime we lose our peace, forgiveness will restore our peace. Negative emotions create barriers in our heart that separate us from God and others. God conveys us into His kingdom when we are saved. Any area with a negative emotion is under enemy control. Forgiveness always transports us back into God's territory.

> *He [God] has delivered us from the power of darkness and conveyed us into the kingdom of the Son of His love, in whom we have redemption through His blood, the forgiveness of sins* (Colossians 1:13-14).

### Interruptions in Peace

When we begin to practice connecting with Christ through dropping down, we will sometimes experience interruptions in our connection. If we feel any negative emotion, we have lost our peace. When we lose our peace, we can no longer feel the presence of God. But don't be worried. The antidote for any toxic emotion is forgiveness and/or release. Occasionally we simply need to release a person or situation into the hands of God.

If the interruption was just a mere temptation that briefly distracted us, causing us to lose a sense of God's presence, we can simply release it from the gut and we'll instantly get our peace back. Suppose your spouse forgets to pick up the dry cleaning and you feel irritated; you can release it to God right away and get your peace back immediately. If you get angry and dwell on it for even a few minutes, you will need to release forgiveness. If we behave badly, we need to receive forgiveness. If we ever wonder whether it is a mere temptation or a sin, we should forgive. We can never forgive too much. When in doubt, forgive. As soon as we drop down and allow Christ the forgiver to cleanse us, our peace returns every time.

*We can't forgive too much!*

This God-tool of forgiveness is not a principle but an encounter with the Prince of Peace Himself, Christ the forgiver within you. God is the One who forgives, and He lives and abides within each of us. When we need to extend or receive forgiveness, we simply allow Him to go to any toxic emotion in us.

There is internal evidence verifying that forgiveness has taken place—the negative emotion changes to supernatural peace. Forgiveness is not complete if we still feel the unpleasant emotion. That is how we know that we did it right. If in doubt, we only need to close our eyes and think of the person or event that was associated with the negative emotion. Peace where there was once pain means that we truly forgave. If hurt, fear, lust, anger, guilt, or shame is still there, we need to forgive. To experience forgiveness, we let Christ in us go to the pain, anxiety, or any other toxic emotion and He washes it away. Forgiveness is like a beautiful love river that washes out toxins from our hearts and replaces them with the peace of God.

Watching Dennis minister, it didn't take too long for me (Jen) to see that the Holy Spirit worked according to certain patterns and principles. I noticed first of all that God is quite capable of bringing to mind what need He wants to address and the order or sequence in which He chooses to address them. I also noticed that Dennis always followed the lead of the Holy Spirit. When I made notes of the steps of ministry, I simply recorded how the Holy Spirit was working. Neither Dennis nor I "came up with a method." We documented how God works. After all, the Holy Spirit is the minister. Our only job is to allow Him to do the work and to be His facilitators when assisting individuals to whom He is ministering.

God will always save a person who wants to be saved. In the same way, God is always present to forgive. He is always at hand to sanctify a heart presented to Him. Sanctification includes the removal of pain, anger, and fear in our heart through forgiveness. Christ the forgiver works in us and through us, so He does the forgiving whenever we allow Him to. Any toxic emotion in our heart gives a foothold to the enemy. However, the application of forgiveness takes the ground back for God.

*Toxic emotions are an invitation for the enemy.*

As noted previously, because I no longer live but Christ lives in me according to Galatians 2:20, would He ever refuse to love and forgive through me?

## Practice: Steps of Forgiveness

**Prayer.** Close your eyes and get in an attitude of prayer.

**First.** What is the first person or situation God brings to mind—in an image or memory?

**Feel.** Feel the feeling. What is the emotion you feel in your gut?

**Forgive.** Yield your will and let Christ the forgiver flow out toward the person, yourself, or God. You don't forgive a situation; you release it. If a situation came to mind such as a heavy workload, release it into the hands of God from the gut.

Forgiveness can flow to others, ourselves, or to God. Let a river of forgiveness flow to others, drink forgiveness in for yourself (just like when you got saved), and let forgiveness flow out to God. (God didn't do anything wrong, but we must release any judgement against Him to set ourselves free.)

- Christ is the forgiver, so forgiveness works every time.
- Forgiveness is instant, not a process.
- There is no "big or little" offense; forgiveness is all easy for Jesus.

NOTE: Occasionally, you made need one or two additional steps of Fact and Fill in one out of every 30 or 40 emotional healings.

**Fact:** Most emotional wounds do not have a lie attached. Occasionally a lie may be believed at the time of an emotional wounding and become a mental stronghold. Let forgiveness flow first until you have peace, then renounce the lie out loud. Ask the Holy Spirit for the truth (fact) and allow it to be written on your heart. Receive it and drink it in.

**Fill:** If there was an emotional need that wasn't met, such as love or attention, forgive first, then release (use the God-tool of releasing) demands on people and receive filling from the Holy Spirit.

## 3. LOVING

The third function of the human spirit is loving. Love is the most powerful force in the universe. When we open the door of our heart, a river of love can flow out, changing the atmosphere and blessing others. Love is our God-tool released in loving intercession for people, in worship to God, in compassion for miracles, and the motivation for righteous deeds.

To love in the Spirit, simply picture somebody you love and then, allow a river of love to flow from your belly toward them. We don't need words to release supernatural love to someone. However, when we do add words, they will carry an anointing *of love*. Loving intercession should be an experience happening within us, flowing outward from our heart. We sow good deeds or finances the same way. When we release love from our heart while we are sowing, our "seeds" are transformed from the natural into the supernatural.

> *The love of God is the most powerful force in the universe.*

We can let love flow in various expressions:

### Loving Intercession

*Therefore I exhort first of all that supplications, prayers, intercessions, and giving of thanks be made for all men (1 Timothy 2:1).*

## Worship

*For we are the circumcision, who worship God in the Spirit, rejoice in Christ Jesus, and have no confidence in the flesh* (Philippians 3:3).

## Compassion for Miracles

*And when Jesus went out He saw a great multitude; and He was moved with compassion for them, and healed their sick* (Matthew 14:14).

## Righteousness (Obedience Motivated by the Love of God)

*The marriage of the Lamb [at last] has come, and His bride has prepared herself. She has been permitted to dress in fine* (radiant) *linen, dazzling and white—for the fine linen is* (signifies, represents) *the righteousness* (the upright, just, and godly living, deeds, and conduct, and right standing with God) *of the saints* (God's holy people) (Revelation 19:7-8 AMPC).

### Practice

**Prayer.** Close your eyes and get in an attitude of prayer.

**Loving Intercession.** Without words, yield to Christ within and let a river of loving intercession flow out to any person who comes to mind.

**Worship.** Without words, release a river of grateful worship toward God.

**Compassion:** Allow a river of compassion to flow out to someone in need.

**Righteous Deeds.** Allow the Lord to show you something He wants you to do. Do it later, letting a river of anointing flow while doing it.

## 4. RELEASING

The fourth loving function is releasing from our belly and is similar to forgiveness. When we release we're not forgiving a particular person but giving them to God. If we feel anxious about someone or something, we should release it into the hands of God until we feel peace. Why? Because we have entrusted it to God, we are no longer carrying the burden ourselves. Jesus invites us to this place of rest:

> *Come to Me, all you who labor and are heavy laden, and I will give you rest. Take My yoke upon you and learn from Me, for I am gentle and lowly in heart, and you will find rest for your souls. For My yoke is easy and My burden is light* (Matthew 11:28-30).

When we learn to release from our heart, we give people and circumstances to the Lord. It is like an internal Jubilee. We are placing our problems into the hands of a loving, capable God who is able to do what He knows is best. He takes them because we've entrusted them to Him. When we hang on to things, our willpower actually hinders God. Release is our God-tool for giving control back to Him. God is in charge of the universe. He is in charge of people, circumstances, timing, children, spouses, promotions, and demotions. When you release, you place people and circumstances back into the hands of God.

*Jesus invites us to enter His rest.*

### People

> *They are God's servants, not yours. They are responsible to Him, not to you. Let Him tell them whether they are right or wrong. And God is able to make them do as they should* (Romans 14:4 TLB).

*Circumstances*

*He went a little farther and fell on His face, and prayed, saying, "O My Father, if it is possible, let this cup pass from Me; nevertheless, not as I will, but as You will* (Matthew 26:39).

*Possessions*

*"If you want to give it all you've got," Jesus replied, "go sell your possessions; give everything to the poor. All your wealth will then be in heaven. Then come follow me." That was the last thing the young man expected to hear. And so, crest-fallen, he walked away. He was holding on tight to a lot of things, and he couldn't bear to let go* (Matthew 19:21-22 MSG).

### Practice

**Prayer.** Close your eyes and get in an attitude of prayer.

**First.** Think of a person or situation that causes you to feel tense, anxious, or stressed.

**Feel.** Feel the feeling.

**Release.** Release it into the hands of God until you feel peace.

## 5. RESISTING

The fifth loving function of the human spirit is resisting. There is a right way to resist and a wrong way. The following chapter explains the function of resisting in greater depth. The wrong way to resist, and many believers do this, is to put up a wall or close the door of our heart when we encounter someone we would prefer to avoid. When we become tense in our gut, we put up a wall with our willpower. We can try to fake it by smiling and talking to them, but inwardly we are protecting ourselves. "The wall" is flesh and is birthed out of fear. Fear belongs to the enemy's kingdom, so he can easily penetrate a willpower wall.

If we shouldn't resist with willpower, what is the correct way to resist? Supernatural peace! God has given us the capacity to resist negative atmospheres around us by allowing Him to guard us with His peace. We can feel a negative atmosphere around us while experiencing peace in our heart. We bear witness to outside pressure but don't take it in. Instead of putting up a wall, we yield to Christ within. As soon as we feel the peace of His presence in our heart, we are in a place of safety because *"He Himself is our peace"* (Eph. 2:14). Remember, the enemy can't touch the fruit of the Spirit!

> *The peace of God, which surpasses all understanding, will guard your hearts and minds through Christ Jesus* (Philippians 4:7).

In a hostile environment or when you are in the presence of an angry person, drop down and let the peace of God guard your heart and your mind. Remember, we don't open our heart to the person; we open our heart to Christ in us. That way Jesus "stands" between us and any person who might confront us. When Jesus guards us, we can resist successfully.

*The enemy can't touch the fruit of the Spirit.*

## NOTE

1.  For more information on this subject, we offer *Five Functions of the Human Spirit* as a booklet as well as CD and DVD sets on our website, www.forgive123.com.

*Chapter 9*

# Battle for Our Will

As mentioned previously, resisting is one of the functions of our human spirit. Have you ever noticed that when you are listening to a nervous public speaker you can begin to get anxious for them? You are actually picking up something unpleasant they are releasing into the atmosphere. However, if you dropped down to peace in your spirit it would be impossible for you to feel nervous. We can resist negative emotional influences in the atmosphere around us as well as pressure from demonic activity.

## Our Will Is the Prize

Our behavior is determined by whatever controls our will. When a mother hears her child cry, she rushes to see what is wrong because her heart is moved by compassion. If we are thirsty, we choose to drink water or some other beverage. Our will has been "engaged" for action.

Both God and the devil want our will so they can express their nature through us. God works from the *inside* to get our will. The Lord wants us to be expressions of Him on the earth. First God *connects* with our spirit. Next, through the process of sanctification, He *owns* more and more of our heart. Finally, He *expresses* His nature through us. Some Christians are very consecrated and obedient to God while others hardly allow their Christianity to influence their lives at all. Jesus modeled a life that *fully* represented Father God. He told Philip, *"He who has seen me has seen the Father"* (John 14:9).

---

*If our will is not engaged*
*we do nothing.*

---

*Do you not know that if you continually surrender yourselves to anyone to do his will, you are the slaves of him whom you obey, whether that be to sin, which leads to death, or to obedience which leads to righteousness* (right standing with God)? (Romans 6:16 AMPC)

The devil works from the *outside* to try to get our will. He craves bodies through which he can manifest his evil nature. Just as there are different levels of Christian commitment, there are different levels of demonic influence, ranging from mild harassment to full possession. The Gadarene demoniac was demon possessed (Mark 5:1–5; Luke 8:26–39). How did this happen? First, the demonic realm made a *connection*. Then the man from Gadara *owned* the demonic influence as part of himself. Finally, the demons freely *expressed* their personalities through him.

---

*Both God and the devil want our will.*

---

Both God and the devil want to express themselves through us and accomplish their plans and purposes on earth. Jesus set the example for us during His earth walk when He lived as the representative of His heavenly Father. He expressed the will of Father God perfectly in the life that He lived, the words that He spoke, the deeds that He did, and the death that He died.

> *The word which you hear is not Mine but the Father's who sent Me* (John 14:24).

> *Most assuredly, I say to you, the Son can do nothing of Himself, but what He sees the Father do; for whatever He does, the Son also does in like manner* (John 5:19).

God's nature is love and He desires to bring redemption to humankind on earth. God has a divine plan, but He works through people to implement His will. Jesus finished the assignment given Him by His Father (see John 17:4), and He Himself became a Father to a new race of men—born-again believers. In turn, the Lord has appointed righteous deeds for us to do in the power of His grace. God's will is always perfectly expressed in heaven as a flow of divine purpose. When we yield our will to the will of God, He releases heaven on earth through us. Therefore, the work begun by Jesus is carried on through believers today.

> *For we are His workmanship, created in Christ Jesus for good works, which God prepared beforehand that we should walk in them* (Ephesians 2:10).

> ### *Yielding our will to God releases heaven on earth.*

The devil's nature is marked by fear and hatred, and he wants to bring destruction and death to us. He takes people captive to fulfill his evil plans on earth. Paul exhorts Timothy to correct those who have been caught in *"the snare of the devil, having been taken captive by him to do his will"* (2 Tim. 2:26).

## FREE WILL

Many individuals have a serious misconception about the meaning of "free will." Our will is not an independent agent. We have a free will only to the extent that we can choose to obey one of two laws—the law of the Spirit of life in Christ Jesus, or the law of sin and death (see Rom. 8:2). Our will does not have the option to be "neutral" or uncommitted. The Scriptures say we become the slave *"of the one we obey"* (see Rom. 6:16 NIV). We serve God and do His will, or we serve the devil to do his will.

Have you ever wondered why certain people choose to destroy their lives with drugs or alcohol? Despite all evidence to the contrary, they will insist they are doing it because they *want to!* They are actually being controlled by *"the prince of the power of the air"* (Eph. 2:2). The only thing truly in our control is how much of us God owns or how much the devil owns.

> *You once walked according to the course of this world, according to the prince of the power of the air, the spirit who now works in the sons of disobedience, among whom also we all once conducted ourselves in the lusts of our flesh, fulfilling the desires of the flesh and of the mind, and were by nature children of wrath, just as the others* (Ephesians 2:2-3).

*Thoughts prompt us.*
*Emotions motivate us.*
*Our will generates behavior.*

A certain disciple of Jesus named Dorcas was commended for doing the will of God expressed in many *"good works and charitable deeds"* (see Acts 9:36). When she passed away suddenly, the believers called for Peter, weeping and showing him all the tunics and garments she had made for them. Peter was so moved that he prayed for her to be raised from the dead—and she was! Dorcas expressed the love of God in good deeds.

Enoch became so radically possessed by God that the earth could not hold him and God took him up to heaven (see Gen. 5:24).

> *Because of faith Enoch was caught up and transferred to heaven, so that he did not have a glimpse of death; and he was not found, because God had translated him. For even before he was taken to heaven, he received testimony [still on record] that he had pleased and been satisfactory to God* (Hebrews 11:5 AMPC).

Consider again the Gadarene demoniac. Jesus and His disciples crossed the Sea of Galilee and came to the region of Gadara. As soon as they got out of the boat they encountered the demon-possessed man who appeared wildly insane:

> *And when He had come out of the boat, immediately there met Him out of the tombs a man with an unclean spirit, who had his dwelling among the tombs; and no one could bind him, not even with chains, because he had often been bound with shackles and chains. And the chains had been pulled apart by him, and the shackles broken in pieces; neither could anyone tame him. And always, night and day, he was in the mountains and in the tombs, crying out and cutting himself with stones* (Mark 5:2–5).

If the demoniac was not manifesting his human nature, who was being expressed through him? The Scriptures tell us that evil spirits were expressing themselves through this man. He was *possessed* by evil.

When Jesus commanded the evil spirits to come out of him, they spoke and said they were *"legion"* (Mark 5:10). In the time of Jesus, a Roman legion made up an entire army of around 5,000 soldiers.

Soon the townsfolk arrived and they found *"the one who had been demon-possessed and had the legion, sitting and clothed and in his right mind"* (Mark 5:15). He was no longer under the control of demons.

## CONNECT, OWN, EXPRESS

God desires to work in and through His people. The Lord wants to *connect* with us, *own* us, and *express* His nature through us. We are His purchased possession for that very reason.

> *Do you not know that your body is the temple of the Holy Spirit who is in you, whom you have from God, and you are not your own? For you were bought at a price* (1 Corinthians 6:19-20).

> *I beseech you therefore, brethren, by the mercies of God, that you present your bodies a living sacrifice, holy, acceptable to God, which is your reasonable service* (Romans 12:1).

When we live a yielded life, we are transformed more and more into the image of Christ. The more He owns of us, the more He can express His nature through us. Paul prayed that God would strengthen us in our inner man so Christ would dwell in our hearts through faith.

> *May Christ through your faith [actually] dwell* (settle down, abide, make His permanent home) *in your hearts! May you be rooted deep in love and founded securely on love, that you may have the power and be strong to apprehend and grasp with all the saints [God's devoted people, the experience of that love] what is the breadth and length and height and depth [of it]; [that you may really come] to know [practically, through experience for yourselves] the love of Christ, which far*

*surpasses mere knowledge [without experience]; that you may be filled [through all your being] unto all the fullness of God [may have the richest measure of the divine Presence, and become a body wholly filled and flooded with God Himself]!* (Ephesians 3:17–19 AMPC)

> *God's Goal: Connect → Own → Express*
> *The Enemy's Goal: Connect → Own → Express*

The enemy also wants bodies in which to live. Evil spirits want to *connect* with us, *own* us, and *express* their nature through us. The devil wants to express himself through us. Evil spirits try to control our thoughts, words, and behavior. The Gadarene demoniac was fully demon-possessed. Demons had such power in his life that he no longer resembled a human being. Evil spirits had connected with him, owned his will, and freely expressed their evil personalities through him.

## SELF-DELIVERANCE

Martin Luther (1483–1546), German monk, theologian, and seminal figure of the Protestant Reformation, restored the truth of the "priesthood of the believer" to the church. Prior to Luther, believers were divided into two classes—secular and spiritual. Therefore, believers were made dependent upon Catholic priests for interpreting the Bible, for confession of sin, exorcism, and all other spiritual functions. Luther said:

> How then if they are forced to admit that we are all equally priests, as many of us as are baptized, and by this way we truly are; while to them is committed only the Ministry (ministerium Predigtamt) and consented to by us (nostro consensu)? If they recognize this they would

know that they have no right to exercise power over us (ius imperii, in what has not been committed to them) except insofar as we may have granted it to them, for thus it says in 1 Peter 2:9, "You are a chosen race, a royal priesthood, a priestly kingdom." In this way we are all priests, as many of us as are Christians.[1]

> *We are all priests unto God.*

Unfortunately, although Luther proclaimed truth, few believers today are functioning in their full spiritual potential. Happily that day is coming to an end, and the Lord is proclaiming now is the time for believers to be equipped so they can take their places in the Army of the Lord.

Through Christ the deliverer within, we can do self-deliverance. We don't have to go to an "expert" for deliverance. When we yield to the authority of Christ the deliverer, He rises up to displace evil hitchhikers. When we submit to God and get peace inside, we have already won the victory. After we take back legal ground from the enemy, he has to flee from us.

> *Therefore submit to God. Resist the devil and he will flee from you* (James 4:7).

## RESISTING THE ENEMY

When my son, Jason, was a young boy, I (Dennis) felt strong irritation in the atmosphere of our usually peaceful home. Suddenly, an ape-like demon with an ugly face manifested right before my eyes. When I commanded it to go, it vanished through the closed front door in a flash. Because I heard my son crying, I went to check on him. "What's wrong?" I asked.

"Something's trying to make me hate you and Mommy, but I don't want to!"

I asked, "Did you see it?"

"Yes!"

"What did it look like?"

"Bigfoot!"

My first thought was, "That's not what I saw because it was only three feet tall," not realizing that a child might not be aware of Bigfoot's height.

Jason had seen it before because he had drawn a picture of it. He pulled a drawing from his desk. My son is quite a good artist, and the drawing looked exactly like what I had seen. Fortunately, without even knowing what he was doing, Jason had successfully resisted by refusing to give in to the anger.

The Holy Spirit in us is far more powerful than anything that can come against us.[2] With peace in our heart, we can resist any negative atmosphere whether flesh or spirit. We should be atmosphere changers rather than products of our environment. If we accidentally take something in, however, all we have to do is receive forgiveness and we'll get our peace back right away.

> *A willpower wall is fear*
> *and fails to protect us.*

There is a right way and a wrong way to resist. The most common way believers try to resist is the wrong way—putting up a wall. However, that "wall" is flesh, which is a carnal weapon (see 2 Cor. 10:4).Allowing the supernatural peace of God to be our protection is the right way to resist. The Scriptures tell us that *"He Himself is our*

SELF-DELIVERANCE MADE SIMPLE

*peace"* (Eph. 2:14). When we yield to Christ within, we feel the peace of His presence.

The next time you are in a hostile environment, drop down and yield to God in your heart. It may feel like you are vulnerable because you are more accustomed to putting up a wall. However, we are not opening to a person or outside environment; we are opening up our heart to Christ within, trusting Him to protect us. When God is in control, His peace guards our heart and mind (see Phil. 4:7).

> ### Peace guards our heart and mind.

Finally, resist the enemy. If you have peace inside and feel a bad atmosphere outside—such as depression, fear, chaos, or anger—don't take it in. The enemy can't come in a door you won't open. Yield to the peace of God in your heart while resisting the outside atmosphere. It is like having a spiritual screen door. You can feel the breeze, but insects can't come in. If you give in by accident, receive forgiveness and you will get your peace back instantly.

## Two Vital Principles

### 1. *The Principle of Resistance*

Jesus was *led* by the Holy Spirit into the wilderness where He resisted the devil. In the army, every soldier must go to boot camp before being successful on the battlefield. The Lord wants us to grow spiritually. He purposely allows times of testing to make us strong.

> *Then Jesus, being filled with the Holy Spirit, returned from the Jordan and was led by the Spirit into the wilderness, being tempted for forty days by the devil* (Luke 4:1-2a).

## 2. *The Principle of Empowerment*

After Jesus prevailed in His great temptation in the presence of Satan, He came out of the wilderness in the *power* of the Spirit. Resistance builds spiritual strength.

> *Then Jesus returned in the power of the Spirit to Galilee, and news of Him went out through all the surrounding region. ..."The Spirit of the Lord is upon Me, because He has anointed Me to preach the gospel to the poor; He has sent Me to heal the brokenhearted, to proclaim liberty to the captives and recovery of sight to the blind, to set at liberty those who are oppressed"* (Luke 4:14, 18).

## REVIEW OF SELF-DELIVERANCE

We don't have to go to an "expert" for deliverance. Through Christ the deliverer within, we can accomplish self-deliverance. When we submit to God and get peace inside, we have already won the victory. As we take back ground from the enemy, he must flee from us. Self-deliverance includes three key steps.

First, we must be in the place of peace. Toxic emotions must be replaced with supernatural peace. If you recognize an area in which you are being attacked, in an attitude of prayer ask the Lord, "Where did this get started?" When you see a person or situation and feel a negative emotion, allow forgiveness to wash it out until you feel peace. The enemy has now lost permission to stay.

When we take back ground from the enemy, deliverance is usually automatic. However, we can also yield to Christ the deliverer in us and welcome Him to fill us head to toe and radiate out to "push out" any tormenting spirit. Occasionally we must verbally rebuke the enemy and command him to go.

## Keep your peace.

Second, resist the outside atmosphere. The enemy can't get through a door you won't open. Yield to peace in your heart but resist the outside atmosphere. If you have peace inside and feel a bad atmosphere outside—such as depression, fear, chaos, or anger—don't take it in. If you give in to it by accident, receive forgiveness and get your peace back.

Third, guard your thoughts and emotions. The enemy tries to connect with you through two doors—the mind door or the emotion door. Remember, the enemy works from the outside to get your will. If you have peace, you are safe. Don't own all the thoughts that you hear in your head. If you hear a thought that doesn't sound like something God would say, don't accept it. It doesn't matter if the devil or your flesh says it—don't take it if God doesn't give it.

If you have peace in your heart but still feel pressure, yield to Christ the deliverer in you and welcome Him to fill you from head to toe. As you yield to Him, allow His presence to radiate outward, pushing back anything oppressive in the atmosphere.

When we drop down and allow peace to guard our heart, we increase in spiritual prowess, or strength and skill. You may fail at times, but what do you do when you fail? You forgive and receive forgiveness. Allow the Forgiver to restore your peace. As we allow the Lord to rule our heart, we cultivate patience and hope.

## Make Jesus Lord of your heart.

When you become more proficient in exercising the five functions of your spirit, you will notice your spiritual strength increases. Things that once caused you to have a meltdown or greatly irritated you will eventually be slight annoyances that you easily release. Ever-increasing peace will be a way of life.

## NOTES

1.  *De captivitate Babylonica ecclesiae praeludium* [*Prelude concerning the Babylonian Captivity of the church*], Weimar Ausgabe 6, 564.6–14 as quoted in Norman Nagel, "Luther and the Priesthood of All Believers," Concordia Theological Quarterly 61 (October 1997) 4:283-84.

2.  See Chapter 8, "Five Functions of the Human Spirit."

*Chapter 10*

# RESISTING TEMPTATION

## BY DENNIS

To successfully resist temptation we must understand the enemy and how he works so we can *"stand against the wiles of the devil"* (Eph. 6:11). Just as we can learn to resist a negative atmosphere, we can also learn to resist temptation before we sin. If we do sin, of course, the remedy is forgiveness and repentance. However, there is a better way. When we understand how the enemy works to ensnare us and know how to use the God-tools we've been given, we can live in ever-increasing freedom.

> *Be sober, be vigilant; because your adversary the devil walks about like a roaring lion, seeking whom he may devour. Resist him* (1 Peter 5:8-9a).

> *We use our powerful God-tools for...fitting every loose thought and emotion and impulse into the structure of life shaped by Christ. Our tools are ready at hand for clearing the ground of every obstruction and building lives of obedience into maturity* (2 Corinthians 10:5-6 MSG).

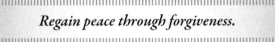

*Regain peace through forgiveness.*

## DIVINE MAGNETISM

We cannot come to God unless He first draws us to Himself. Therefore, His love is magnetic. Jesus tells us, *"No one can come to Me unless the Father who sent Me draws him"* (John 6:44). This is true before we are saved as well as after. The Lord never stops drawing us closer to Himself. What is our part in the matter? We must cooperate by yielding to Him. Every time we come to God in prayer, He is there for us as our Immanuel, or *"God with us"* (Matt. 1:23). When we yield, we can sense the gentle "pull" of His presence wooing us ever closer to Himself. The Lord initiates and we respond. We draw close...and He draws closer still.

*Draw nigh to God, and he will draw nigh to you* (James 4:8 KJV).

When the Lord took me to the school of the Spirit, He taught me that peace was my assurance that I was connected to His presence, or joined to Him. When I was communing with the Lord in prayer, I felt peace. If someone came to mind and I felt a toxic emotion in my gut, I could no longer feel God's presence. Every time I forgave, I instantly experienced peace again. The Lord admonished me by saying, "Dennis, don't let anything come between what you and I have together."

*Don't let anything come between you and God.*

Animal predators go after easy targets whenever possible. They don't attack the herd but go after stragglers. When we walk in the

Spirit, we are protected by God because *"he who is joined to the Lord is one spirit with Him"* (1 Cor. 6:17). Having a church family also adds greatly to our protection. The Scriptures encourage us:

> *Let us consider one another in order to stir up love and good works, not forsaking the assembling of ourselves together, as is the manner of some* (Hebrews 10:24-25).

> *God sets the solitary in families* (Psalm 68:6).

## DRAWN AWAY

The enemy attempts to draw us away from the Lord to make us easy prey. If we engage in sin or get in the flesh, we draw away from Christ within. I pictured my "bucket" going up and moving away from Christ within.[1] When our focus is no longer on Christ in us, our five natural senses begin to rule instead of Jesus. Separation from the Lord makes us vulnerable to the appetites and passions of the flesh, the temptations of the world, and the devices of the enemy.

> *Each one is tempted when he is drawn away by his own desires and enticed* (James 1:14).

As a result, I learned the principle of prompt obedience and dealt quickly with any internal disruptions because I didn't want to have my communion with Jesus interrupted for any reason. Because of this, I made forgiveness a lifestyle.

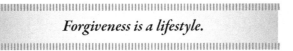

*Forgiveness is a lifestyle.*

## PROMPT OBEDIENCE

Jesus rescued me out of a life of drugs and ruin. I got saved late one night when I turned on the television and began to mock a preacher on a Christian program. Suddenly he pointed his finger at the camera and said, "Jesus can change *your* life!" His words pierced my heart and I felt he was speaking directly to me. I bowed my head and prayed, "Jesus, I'm a sinner. I need you to come into my life and help straighten out the terrible mess I've made."

I meant it; I never was so sincere about anything in my life! Unbelievable! I found myself taking a bag of marijuana over to the sink and dumping it down the garbage disposal. All the while, a voice inside me kept protesting, "Don't do it! Don't you realize that grass cost a lot of money? What's the matter with you?" Nevertheless, I dumped the stuff and listened to the disposal grind it up because I knew it was the right thing to do. I'd asked, and the Lord began to show me how to start cleaning up my act immediately!

Something else started working in me—something not visible to the naked eye. The Lord began to cleanse the sins of my heart—the secret sins. I found out as I prayed and read the Bible that I was packed full of sins. Most of my waking hours were spent confessing one sin or another or forgiving other people. I was amazed at what a full-time job it was!

When the Lord first taught me about peace and forgiveness, I was overjoyed! I could live in constant communion with God. The Carmelite monk Brother Lawrence (1614–1691), who practiced the presence of God, became my mentor.[2] I longed to walk with the Lord in the same way. However, at first I discovered it was very difficult for me as I tried to keep short accounts with God. It seemed like I had to receive forgiveness for ungodly thoughts or forgive others who annoyed or wounded me every few minutes! I thought in despair, "How can I even go to work and get anything done?"

Even though my focus initially caused me to bounce up and down like a yo-yo, I soon learned the principle of persevering in forgiveness. I found it was hard at times, but when I blew it I knew He wanted me to get up and try again. It was as though Someone was encouraging me from within. I was determined to master this exercise of forgiveness and stay right with God.

*For a righteous man may fall seven times and rise again* (Proverbs 24:16).

Fortunately, I noticed that the intervals between instances of forgiving grew farther and farther apart. I was gaining spiritual strength, and soon I was able to resist the temptation to react. Even baby steps of obedience build spiritual authority! I found I could just "let it go" before I sinned. If a coworker annoyed me and I began to feel tension in my gut, I could drop down to my spirit and release it to God before I lost my temper or blurted out something harsh.

> *Baby steps of obedience build spiritual authority!*

The principle of prompt obedience proved to be an effective tool of resistance. Do what God tells you to do quickly and don't listen to other voices.

The enemy wasn't hiding when I was first saved. The temptations became blatant! My former drug dealer came by to offer me free drugs. Cute waitresses flirted shamelessly with me. Married women propositioned me. Temptation was suddenly everywhere. I discovered that there is not only a Savior who loves me and gave His life for me, but there is a tempter always lurking close by, attempting to destroy my life. I was the target of an enemy other than myself, but prompt obedience to God kept me out of the devil's traps.

*Submit yourselves...to God. Resist the devil, and he will flee from you* (James 4:7).

## TWO SPIRITUAL LAWS

Our will is free only in that we have a choice between two spiritual laws to obey—the law of sin and death or the law of life in Christ Jesus. *"Do you not know that to whom you present yourselves slaves to obey, you are that one's slaves whom you obey, whether of sin leading to death, or of obedience leading to righteousness?"* (Rom. 6:16). There is no neutral territory for the human will. We can only choose which law to obey.

1. The Law of Sin and Death

2. The Law of the Spirit of Life in Christ Jesus

In the early years of my Christian life, I didn't always deal with sin quickly. From time to time, I indulged in some "spiritual temper tantrums" lasting for hours or even days. I noticed that this caused an increasing sense of distance with God as well as adversely affecting my daily life, my family, and my work. When we emanate a bad atmosphere, it has a ripple effect. The longer my bad attitude persisted, the worse it got for me.

The Lord taught me that I had entered into the Law of Sin and Death, which strengthens flesh. Those things we sow take root, grow, and produce a harvest. *"Whatever a man sows, that he will also reap"* (Gal. 6:7). The longer we let it remain, the more abundant the poisonous harvest will be.

> *The temptation to give in to evil comes from us and only us. We have no one to blame but the leering, seducing flare-up of our own lust. Lust gets pregnant, and has a baby: sin! Sin grows up to adulthood, and becomes a real killer* (James 1:15 MSG)

### *Obedience builds spiritual muscle.*

On the other hand, when we forgive quickly or act in prompt obedience to God, we walk in the Spirit and live via the Law of the Spirit of Life in Christ Jesus. Prompt obedience strengthens our spirit. The *"law of the Spirit of life in Christ Jesus has made me free from the law of sin and death"* (Rom. 8:2). We gain spiritual muscle through obedience. It becomes easier and easier to obey God.

## THE PRINCIPLE OF POWER

Proper focus is a major element of faith. That is why staying in communion with God is so important for living a victorious Christian life. The story in the Gospels of Peter walking on water is a perfect illustration (see Matt. 14:22–33). Jesus sent His disciples out on a boat to cross to the other side of the Sea of Galilee. When the boat was in the middle of the sea, a strong wind arose and they began to fight heavy waves.

As if that weren't bad enough, in the wee hours of the morning they were terrified to see a figure walking on the water toward them. Jesus called out to comfort them. Peter boldly cried out, *"Master, if it's really you, call me to come to you on the water"* (Matt. 14:28 MSG). Jesus said, "Come on." Peter climbed out of the boat and began to walk to Jesus...until he took his eyes off Him and looked around at the tossing waves. Fear gripped Peter's heart and he immediately began to sink into the sea. As soon as Peter cried out, "Save me!" Jesus reached out, grabbed his hand, and rebuked him saying, "Why did you begin to doubt, you of little faith!"

> *Proper focus is a major*
> *element of faith.*

When we stay in the supernatural peace of God, the Lord is always present to guide us and keep us safe. If we become afraid, we stray into the wrong kingdom. God never leaves us even if our own heart wanders away from Him. God has already given us an effective antidote for fear—trusting in Him. As soon as we turn back to the Lord we find Him, and our peace is restored.

*He shall not be afraid of evil tidings: his heart is fixed, trusting in the Lord* (Psalm 112:7 KJV).

## *Supernatural peace keeps us safe.*

When I was still a relatively new believer, the Lord was prompting me to plant a church. However, I came down with a severe case of pneumonia and had to be rushed to the hospital. It was so bad that the doctors feared I was dying. I was hallucinating and the enemy began to shout, "You're going to die!" From within my heart, however, a faint, squeaky voice said, "You shall live and not die!" (See Psalm 118:17.)

Although very ill and extremely weak, I chose to focus on the voice of God in me and not the words of the enemy. God often speaks to us in the *"still small voice"* (see 1 Kings 19:11–13). I noticed that when I listened to the Lord, His voice grew louder and louder while that of the enemy became weaker and weaker. As I continued to focus on the words of life, my health was supernaturally restored, surprising friends and family as well as the medical professionals attending me.

Later, the Lord assured me that the enemy is just a "rat with a loudspeaker." But we serve a big, big God! The Lord is our authority, and His voice is the only one to whom we should listen. When Jesus, our Shepherd, calls us, we must follow Him and flee from the voice of a stranger (see John 10:4-5). When we focus on Jesus, He strengthens us with His power!

*He who is in you is greater than he who is in the world* (1 John 4:4).

> *We give power to what we
> give attention to!*

## PRACTICE MAKES...PERMANENT

The old saying "practice makes perfect" is only a partial truth. We can practice giving in to our flesh or obeying the Holy Spirit. Those things that we practice regularly tend to become permanent parts of our life. When we become determined to make forgiveness and peace a lifestyle, peace will become a reality.

> *But those who wait on the Lord shall renew their strength; they shall mount up with wings like eagles, they shall run and not be weary, they shall walk and not faint* (Isaiah 40:31).

Even young children and teenagers can learn to walk in the Spirit and resist temptation. Often they become proficient more rapidly than adults because they haven't spent a lifetime exercising their flesh. I (Dennis) prayed with a 13-year-old girl named Ariel who was being bullied at school by a group of girls who had pretended to be her friends. On one occasion they told her they were having a party then didn't invite her. I taught Ariel how to pray through the pain of rejection by yielding to Christ the forgiver within, and she felt much better after her emotional pain was replaced by peace.

However, after some time passed, her mother called and said the girls continued to wound Ariel regularly in a variety of ways. I prayed with her again, but this time gave her a strategy to break out of a victim mentality. Even though we forgive and get peace, in an ongoing situation we can forgive over and over again without getting complete victory. We need a new mindset to go from victim to victor.

---

*Go from victim to victor.*

---

Ariel began to let love flow out to the girls at school, even while they were saying unkind words. In this way she was able to take up the *"shield of faith"* which quenches *"the fiery darts of the wicked one"* (Eph. 6:16). Nothing can penetrate the peace of God. Because God can guide us when we are at peace, the Lord then drew Ariel's attention to several girls sitting in a far corner of the cafeteria. She felt led to go sit with them and discovered they were Christians. They became her new best friends!

> *Solid food belongs to those who are of full age, that is, those who by reason of use have their senses exercised to discern both good and evil* (Hebrews 5:14).

---

*Practice makes...permanent!*

---

### NOTES

1.   See Chapter 3.

2.   B. Lawrence, *The Practice of the Presence of God*, (New Kensington, PA: Whitaker House, 1982).

*Chapter 11*

# OVERCOMING FEAR

## BY DR. JEN

Fear, anxiety, and worry have become the common condition of our world today. Far too many individuals lie awake at night tormented by worry. Fear may motivate us and cause us to make bad decisions. We have all had times when fear suddenly paralyzed us or caused our timing to be wrong. Nothing good ever comes from decisions and actions based in fear because we are operating out of the wrong kingdom. Although almost everyone struggles with fear intermittently, for some fear is so constant it becomes part of their personality as a "generalized anxiety disorder."[1]

Fear is not only unpleasant to experience but it invites evil into our life. When we stay in peace we maintain our connection with the kingdom of God, and we have an assurance that *"[God being a partner in their labor] all things work together and are [fitting into a plan] for good to and for those who love God and are called according to [His] design and purpose"* (Rom. 8:28 AMPC). Peace welcomes God's plan for good.

As previously stated, all emotions can be categorized as either love-based or fear-based. In the kingdom of God, all emotions are love-based and are also infused with the light and life of God! Fear, on the other hand, produces darkness and death.

How does fear affect us?

- Fear separates us from the presence of God.

- Fear diminishes us.

- Fear shrinks our world.

- Fear isolates us.

- Fear weighs us down.

- Fear creates pain and torment.

- Fear disconnects us from our true identity.

- Fear steals our destiny.

- Fear gives the enemy permission to harass us.

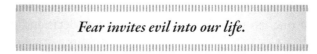

*Fear invites evil into our life.*

God has already given us effective spiritual equipment to triumph over the enemies we face in life. However, we must know how to use our God-tools to wage effective warfare...and that includes dealing with fear.

> *God is strong, and he wants you strong. So take everything the Master has set out for you, well-made weapons of the best materials. And put them to use so you will be able to stand up to everything the Devil throws your way* (Ephesians 6:10 MSG).

## FEAR AND TRUST

Marketers often build brand recognition based on a particular emotion because our emotions motivate us to take action. A brand built on security or trust requires absolute consistency. Why? If a brand claims to be trustworthy but lets customers down, they will instantly turn away and search for a brand that *is* reliable. When we do trust a particular brand, we believe the manufacturer will keep their promises and meet our expectations.

If we trust certain brand names and products, how much more can we rely upon the Lord! God and His Word are always trustworthy. Additionally, He has already given us the *ability* to trust Him. We had to trust the Lord enough to welcome Him into our life and get saved in the first place. Therefore, at any given time, we can trust Him by inviting Him into that moment. How do we know if we have been successful in doing this? We experience supernatural peace! Jesus never takes His gift of peace from us (see John 14:27; John 16:33). We can always tap into the peace of His presence.

*He who dwells in the secret place of the Most High shall abide under the shadow of the Almighty. I will say of the Lord, "He is my refuge and my fortress; my God, in Him I will trust"* (Psalm 91:1-2).

*Look at the lilies of the field and how they grow. They don't work or make their clothing, yet Solomon in all his glory was not dressed as beautifully as they are. And if God cares so wonderfully for wildflowers that are here today and thrown into the fire tomorrow, he will certainly care for you. Why do you have so little faith? So don't worry about these things, saying, "What will we eat? What will we drink? What will we wear?" These things dominate the thoughts of unbelievers, but your heavenly Father already knows all your needs. Seek the Kingdom of God above all else, and live righteously, and he will give you everything you need* (Matthew 6:28–33 NLT).

*Supernatural peace is evidence we trust God.*

Any pocket of fear sabotages our ability to trust. The Bible tells us "do not be afraid" or "fear not" hundreds of times in a variety of ways. The spiritual secret that annihilates fear is trusting God. How do we put that into practice? We receive forgiveness for being afraid and, when necessary, *release* people and circumstances into His hands until we feel peace. God, who is love Himself, will cast out our fear (see 1 John 4:18). Trust in God annihilates fear.

*Trust annihilates fear.*

## HEALING SIMPLE FEAR AND WORRY

Fear and trust are incompatible. They cannot operate simultaneously. Fear is not just an emotion but connects us to a wrong spirit. When we enter into fear, we have taken a step into enemy territory. Many years ago I was going downstairs, and as I turned on the wooden landing halfway down my right foot slipped out from under me. I tumbled down the stairs, stopping only when I crashed into the grandfather clock at the bottom with a thud. I was bruised all over but was very relieved no bones were broken.

Soon afterward I noticed a tiny flutter of fear in my gut whenever I was on stairs, but it was so mild I ignored it. A month or so later my foot slipped again, but I was able to grab hold of the banister. Then Dennis and I went on a ministry trip and we stayed in a room over our host's garage. While I was coming downstairs, I slipped and fell again, but the steps were carpeted and I wasn't hurt. However, it felt almost as though I was...*pushed*!

Soon afterward we returned home. Sure enough, I fell on the stairs again. At this point I decided to get serious about dealing with any fear, no matter how small.

When I took the matter to the Lord in prayer, I could feel a tiny flutter of fear in my gut but couldn't sense any demonic hitchhiker manifesting in the atmosphere. As soon as I received forgiveness for allowing that fear to remain in my heart, my peace was restored.

Ephesians 4:27 tells us to give no place to the devil. Therefore, I received forgiveness for taking in fear and felt it change to peace in my gut. Since that time I haven't felt any fear or fallen when going up or down stairs. As long as I let fear remain, demonic hitchhikers could harass me! This particular incident has made me determined to deal quickly with any fear and refuse to give ground to the enemy.

> *Fear and trust are incompatible.*

I now take fear *very* seriously and refuse to give in to negative headlines or any other worries. God controls the future and orders our steps—when we let Him do so! The only requirement on our part is staying in the right kingdom by letting *"the peace of God rule"* (Col. 3:15).

> *God's Spirit is right alongside helping us along. ...He knows us far better than we know ourselves, knows our...condition, and keeps us present before God. That's why we can be so sure that every detail in our lives of love for God is worked into something good* (Romans 8:26–28 MSG).

**Practice**

**Dealing with simple fear:** Close your eyes in prayer; momentarily feel the fear. Then receive forgiveness until it changes to peace in your gut.

**Dealing with worry:** Close your eyes in prayer and momentarily feel the fear. Receive forgiveness then release people or circumstances into the hands of God until you feel peace.

## GENERALIZED ANXIETY

When Dennis and I were first married, I had such a big problem with fear I felt low-grade anxiety almost all the time. Dennis teased me and called me "little much afraid," a character in the allegory *Hinds' Feet on High Places* by Hannah Hurnard. Fear was such a constant companion that it became generalized fear, flavoring most of my life.

As Dennis prayed with me on a regular basis, one by one my fears simply disappeared. Multiple entry points were healed, and I no longer felt like I was walking on eggshells most of the time. My life became characterized by peace, and I could feel the joy of the Lord instead of constant dread.

Many believers live in an almost constant state of anxiety just like me. When an emotion is *generalized*, you will probably have to pray through several fear issues that form an "emotional cluster." Just take it one at time and enjoy your increasing freedom.

## FEAR AND DESTINY

Even seemingly insignificant wounds can sabotage our destiny. When Dennis and I had been married for about a year, a local church asked him to do a weekend seminar. At that time I was still working a full-time secular job. Incredibly, two days before the seminar, Dennis informed me that I too would be speaking.

In graduate school, debilitating fear of public speaking had made oral presentations a nightmare for me. My skin would become ice cold, and I stumbled over my words. It went much better if I spent up to 20 hours soaking in prayer before speaking. That was quite a bit of time to devote to a short speech or report.

When Dennis told me I'd be speaking at the seminar, my eyes widened in alarm and I blurted out, "Oh, no! I can't! I don't have time to pray 20 hours before then!" Dennis encouraged me that it shouldn't be a problem for me because I already knew the material. After I continued to protest, he informed me that this was an overreaction and told me we were going to pray about it.

Reluctantly, I agreed to pray.

As soon as I closed my eyes, I was surprised to see myself in my mind as a first-grader. Coming in from the playground to use the restroom, I had gotten lost in the halls. I couldn't find the restroom and couldn't find my way back outside to get help from my teacher, so I panicked.

Negative emotions don't go away just because an incident happened a long time ago. They come to the surface as soon as they are triggered. I felt fear in my gut as well as demonic fear in the atmosphere around me. Dennis instructed me to receive forgiveness for taking in that fear. The fear in my gut instantly changed to peace and the oppressive atmosphere lifted. A couple of days later I had a wonderful time speaking at the seminar—without 20 hours of prayer—and have had no trouble in this area ever since.

*Negative emotions can block our destiny.*

What I would have called an insignificant "little" fear would have blocked me from fulfilling a major part of my destiny destiny had it remained. From that time on I never judge any healing as big or little based on my own estimation. God knows exactly what we need to deal with as well as the timing. I also realized that I never would have been able to figure out the source of my problem by myself. It is so much easier to just pray and ask God to reveal where the issue got a foothold—the "entry point."

## Practice

If you have a problem with fear in some area, ask the Lord, "Where did that get started in my life?" If you want the Lord to show you emotional wounds that might block your destiny, inquire in prayer.

**Pray.** Close your eyes and get in an attitude of prayer.

**First.** Focus on the first person or situation that comes to mind.

**Feel.** Feel the feeling that is attached.

**Forgive.** Receive forgiveness or release forgiveness until it changes to peace in your gut.

## HEALING EMOTIONAL TRAUMA

My mother was involved in a terrible car accident when I was in college and, as a result, was too frightened to ever drive again. She passed away many years ago, but what I know now could have set her free. An individual may have a single traumatic experience or several, but it is all easy to deal with through forgiveness. Sometimes forgiveness needs to go three ways—toward another person, ourselves, or to God, if we blame Him for allowing something to happen. We let a river of forgiveness flow toward someone or God and receive it for ourselves as a gift, just like when we welcomed forgiveness at the time of salvation.

Examples of traumatic events include:

- War trauma (PTSI)

- Survivor's guilt

- Car accident

- Sudden death of a loved one

- Home invasions or robbery

- Physical or emotional abuse

- Molestation or rape

- Natural disaster

- Financial setback

- Divorce

Emotional trauma is common. According to statistics provided through the Veterans Administration (VA) at least one serious trauma is experienced during the lifetime of about 50 percent of all women and 60 percent of men. From this group, approximately 20 percent of the women and 8 percent of men develop the symptom cluster identified as Post-Traumatic Stress Injury—PTSI (originally PTSD, or Post-Traumatic Stress Disorder). These numbers are much higher for incidents such as combat exposure, childhood abuse, sexual or physical assault, terrorist attack, serious accident, or natural disaster.

PTSI is defined as a stress-related emotional injury caused by a terrifying event. Common symptoms may include severe anxiety, nightmares, flashbacks, and intrusive and uncontrollable thoughts. In 2011 alone, 476,515 veterans with primary or secondary diagnosis of PTSD received treatment at Department of Veterans Affairs (VA) medical centers and clinics.[2]

Most individuals have been exposed to some frightening events that *could* lead to the symptoms of PTSI but aren't as seriously affected as others. The diagnostic key is symptoms that persist. Experts recommend that a sufferer seek help if the signs last longer than three months. Common reactions to trauma may include:

- Generalized fear and anxiety (hyper-vigilance)

- Sadness or depression

- Anger, irritability, impatience, and sudden rages

- Feelings of guilt or shame

- Unhealthy behavioral changes

Symptoms of PTSI usually begin within three months of the trauma, but may not manifest until years after the event occurred. The four types of diagnostic symptoms included in PTSI are:

*1. Re-experiencing, or reliving, an event through vivid memories*

- Memories triggered by sights, smells, or noises

- Recurrent nightmares about the event

- Vivid flashbacks of the trauma

- Reliving the event for minutes or even days at a time

*2. Emotional numbness*

- Trying to avoid thinking or talking about the experience

- Feeling emotionally numb

- Suppressing emotions or blocking out certain memories

- Losing interest in activities you once enjoyed

- Feeling hopeless about the future

- Having difficulty concentrating

- Suffering from memory problems

- Having trouble maintaining close relationships

*3. Hyper-arousal with chronic feelings of irritability, anger, or nervousness*

- Paranoia in certain situations

- Easily disconcerted or frightened by loud noises

- Feelings of rage and outbursts of anger

- Insomnia
- Seeing or hearing things that aren't there
- Overwhelming guilt or shame
- Self-destructive behavior such as using drugs or drinking too much

### 4. *Avoidance reactions*

- Staying overly busy to avoid thinking
- Avoiding places that are crowded because you fear you can't be "in control"
- Avoiding activities that remind you of the traumatic event

Ordinarily, treatment includes long-term counseling to help individuals cope with their symptoms, often with prescription medications to get some emotional relief. However, God has a faster and more effective way and even wounds from serious traumas can be quickly and permanently healed.

---

### Practice

**Pray.** Close your eyes and pray.

**First.** Picture the traumatic event.

**Feel.** Feel the feeling momentarily.

**Forgive.** Forgive (God, self, and others) until you feel peace.

If you have more than one traumatic issue to deal with, pray through them one at a time. When you feel peace go on to the next thing that comes to mind and deal with it the same way.

---

## REMOVING A FEAR GUARD

### *Two-Headed Dragon*

An old "Garfield the cat" cartoon perfectly illustrates a common spiritual snare of the enemy—the two-headed dragon of fear. In the cartoon, Garfield bolts into a pet shop as a valiant freedom fighter and flings open the cages of the animals while shouting, "You're free! You're free!" However, the terrified cats and dogs cowered in fear and refused to escape from their cages. Garfield muses as he looks around, "Hmmm. Folks must not be heavily into freedom these days." He then slams all the cage doors shut again while shouting, "You're secure! You're secure!"

Unfortunately, we can create our own cages of fear when we believe our fear keeps us safe. Yet God clearly tells us to, "Fear not!"

We were praying with Diana, a young woman who attended our church, and the first thing she pictured was hiding in her bedroom closet as a child while her parents had a knock-down, drag-out fight in the living room. However, she could feel no emotion in her gut, just a sense of numbness. Hiding in fear had become her "strategy" to feel safe from the war going on between her parents.

It is a common defense mechanism for people to put up a wall when they feel threatened, but in this case she was attempting to hide behind one fear—a fear guard—to keep her safe from a bigger fear. That won't keep us safe at all. It's like a two-headed dragon. One head doesn't keep us safe from the other because they are both our enemies. Diana first received forgiveness for using fear as a shield, then she could feel the terror she had felt as a child. Now the core emotion was exposed. She released forgiveness to her parents and instantly felt the safety and comfort of God's presence shielding her from harm.

*You, O Lord, are a shield for me* (Psalm 3:3).

In another prayer session, we ministered to a woman named Sheila. The first person who came to mind was her father. As a child, she had gone into her backyard and was horrified to see the lifeless body of her father dangling from a rope. The situation had been traumatizing, but Sheila only felt numb inside when she pictured the scene of her father's suicide. It was another instance of a fear guard. She received forgiveness for using fear as a form of protection and instantly felt the terror of the situation in her gut. When Sheila released forgiveness to her father and God (because she was angry at God for letting it happen), she felt a deep peace.

A number of years ago, Dennis and I were ministering at a church and the Lord's presence showed up so powerfully that the atmosphere felt as thick as honey. People were lying all over the floor soaking in the anointing, and even the small children were still.

After a while, a woman named Tonya came to the front of the sanctuary where Dennis was sitting on the steps. She sat down next to him with a troubled expression on her face. "What am I missing? Apparently I can't feel what everyone else is feeling." He asked Tonya to close her eyes and pray. The first thing that came to mind was a frightening situation she found herself in as a child. Tonya's panic caused her to make a choice to shut down her feelings out of the fear that she would be overwhelmed. She believed the lie that fear would keep her safe. Tonya had accepted a "fear guard" to rule over her emotions. As soon as the fear guard was gone, she was able to sense the presence of the One who truly keeps us safe.

*Fear is never our guard unless it's the fear of the Lord.*

### Practice

In the case of a fear guard, deliverance precedes healing the emotion. If you picture a frightening situation in prayer and can't feel a negative emotion, receive forgiveness for blocking the emotion first. You should be able to feel the emotion connected to the trauma instantly.

### Practice

**First Fear:** Remove the Fear Guard

**First.** Stay focused on the situation.

**Feel.** Feel the feeling even if you just feel "numb." Numb is a feeling.

**Forgive.** Receive forgiveness for allowing fear to guard you. Now the emotion connected to the trauma can manifest.

**Second Fear:** Heal the Emotional Trauma

**First.** Picture the traumatic situation.

**Feel.** Momentarily feel the feeling you felt when the event happened.

**Forgive.** Forgive God, self, and others until you feel peace.

## NOTES

1. Generalized anxiety disorder (GAD) is an emotional condition characterized by extreme, uncontrollable, irrational worry. Although most people worry when under stress, individuals with GAD continuously feel tense and anxious when there appears to be little to worry about. It often interferes with the ability to function in daily life, as individuals suffering with GAD constantly anticipate disaster even in normal everyday concerns including health, finances, family issues, work difficulties, and so forth. Physical symptoms may include fatigue, headaches, gastrointestinal issues, difficulty concentrating, agitation, insomnia, and twitching. Symptoms must persist for at least six months for a formal diagnosis to be made. GAD affects almost seven million individuals in the United States alone.

2. "Veterans posttraumatic stress disorder," Office of Public Affairs, U. S. Department of Veterans Affairs. Retrieved August 22, 2012 from http://www.va.gov/opa/issues/PTSD .asp.

*Chapter 12*

# SPIRIT OF INSOMNIA

## BY DR. JEN

Opening one eye, I peeked at the clock...again. 11:17 PM. 11:46 PM. 1:15 AM. 2:13 AM. I kept adjusting the pillow, pulling the covers up around my neck, closing my eyes, and shifting to another sleep position. It was the weirdest thing. Usually, as soon as my head hits the pillow I fall asleep—but not tonight. Although I tried to relax, sleep evaded me in the strangest way. I alternated between dropping down to peace then becoming frustrated.

Dennis and I had to leave the mountains of western Massachusetts at 5:00 AM to drive three hours to Boston for a breakfast meeting.

Finally, at 4:00 AM, I dragged myself out of bed after a night with no sleep. After putting on a pot of coffee, I awakened Dennis and we got ready to go. Despite feeling absolutely horrible, I made it through the meeting somehow.

When someone is in traveling ministry, their schedule varies based on the type of speaking engagements they have. It's not a nine to five predictable week followed by a weekend off. A conference may include an evening meeting followed by an early morning session. Sometimes we would be booked for seven days in a row with a mix of morning and evening meetings. When staying in an area for a period of time and driving to multiple locations, we would often have long drives in the car between meetings.

A minister always wants to be at their best so they can focus on the needs of those receiving ministry. Sleepless nights make optimal functioning difficult.

What I didn't know at the time was that this was the beginning of a battle with a *spirit of insomnia*. The lessons we learn from our trials, however, become particularly valuable when we use them to help others. When we are set free, whatever the enemy used to harm us can be turned around and used against him! As far as I am concerned, the sweetest revenge of all against the enemy is to to take what he used against us to help others.

While the reasons for insomnia are varied and sometimes complex, we know the Lord *"gives His beloved sleep"* (Ps. 127:2b).

> *I will both lie down in peace, and sleep; for You alone, O Lord, make me dwell in safety* (Psalm 4:8).

> *When you lie down, you will not be afraid; yes, you will lie down and your sleep will be sweet* (Proverbs 3:24).

Every time the spirit of insomnia attacked me in a different way, I learned new strategies for victory. However, insomnia is not always the result of spiritual warfare. We should begin by being armed with general knowledge as well as practical strategies for combating insomnia.

## SLEEP DEPRIVATION STATISTICS

Statistics about insomnia probably don't mean much for those who can't sleep at night. It's cold comfort to know that more than 25 percent of the American population has bouts of insomnia each year. Around ten percent experience chronic insomnia.[1] One out of every 20 individuals struggle with severe insomnia.[2] "Lack of sleep dramatically affects...health, ability to function, and well-being. Yet, Americans' sleep time over the last century has decreased by 20 [percent]."[3]

## WHAT IS INSOMNIA?

Two main components of insomnia are difficulty sleeping and subsequent impairment of daytime functioning. Individuals who have bouts of insomnia may have trouble falling asleep, staying asleep, or both. They may get too little sleep or their sleep may be poor quality so it doesn't leave them feeling refreshed.[4]

## INSOMNIA AND PHYSICAL HEALTH

Insomnia may interfere with sleep most nights of the week or be an occasional interruption of normal sleep patterns. It can be acute (short-term) or chronic (long-term). *Acute* insomnia may last for one night, a few days, or weeks. Stress at home or work, relational problems, or a traumatic event can cause acute insomnia. *Chronic* insomnia lasts a month or more.

Sleep plays an extremely important role in our physical health. When insomnia becomes a chronic condition, our health suffers. Many chronic diseases are connected to insufficient sleep, and lack of sleep can make existing physical conditions worse.

Sleep is involved in healing and repair of your heart and blood vessels. Ongoing sleep deficiency is linked to an increased risk of heart disease, kidney disease, high blood pressure, diabetes, and stroke. Sleep deficiency also increases the risk of obesity. ...Sleep helps maintain a healthy balance of the hormones that make you feel hungry (ghrelin) or full (leptin). When you don't get enough sleep, your level of ghrelin goes up and your level of leptin goes down. This makes you feel hungrier than when you're well-rested.

Sleep also affects how your body reacts to insulin, the hormone that controls your blood glucose (sugar) level. Sleep deficiency results in a higher than normal blood sugar level, which may increase your risk for diabetes. Sleep also supports healthy growth and development. Deep sleep triggers the body to release the hormone that promotes normal growth in children and teens...[and] also plays a role in puberty and fertility.

Your immune system relies on sleep to stay healthy. This system defends your body against foreign or harmful substances. ...If you're sleep deficient, you may have trouble fighting common infections.[5]

In addition, sleep deprivation can cause chronic, debilitating headaches.[6]

## GOOD SLEEP HYGIENE

It is a good idea to start with common-sense sleep hygiene before tackling other issues. The following sleep tips are adapted from recommendations given by the Mayo Clinic.[7] Start with these simple sleep tips:

1. **Stick to a sleep schedule**. Go to bed and get up at the same time every day, even on weekends, holidays, and days off. Being consistent reinforces your body's sleep-wake cycle and helps promote better sleep at night. There's a caveat, though. If you don't fall asleep within about 15 minutes, get up and do something relaxing. Go back to bed when you're tired. If you agonize over falling asleep, you might find it even tougher to nod off.

2. **Pay attention to what you eat and drink**. Don't go to bed either hungry or stuffed. Your discomfort might keep you up. Also limit how much you drink before bed, to prevent disruptive middle-of-the-night trips to the toilet.

3. **Create a bedtime ritual**. Do the same things each night to tell your body it's time to wind down. This might include taking a warm bath or shower, reading a book, or listening to soothing music—preferably with the lights dimmed. Relaxing activities can promote better sleep by easing the transition between wakefulness and drowsiness. Be wary of using the TV or other electronic devices as part of your bedtime ritual. Some research suggests that screen time or other media use before bedtime interferes with sleep.

4. **Get comfortable**. Create a room that's ideal for sleeping. Often, this means cool, dark and quiet. Consider using room-darkening shades, earplugs, a fan, or other devices to create an environment that suits your needs. Your mattress and pillow can contribute to better sleep, too. As the features of good bedding are subjective, choose what feels most comfortable to you.

5. **Limit daytime naps**. Long daytime naps can interfere with nighttime sleep—especially if you're struggling with insomnia or poor sleep quality at night. If you choose to nap during the day, limit yourself to about 10 to 30 minutes and make it during the midafternoon. If you work nights, you'll need to make an exception to the rules about daytime sleeping.

6. **Include physical activity in your daily routine**. Regular physical activity can promote better sleep, helping you to

fall asleep faster and to enjoy deeper sleep. Timing is important, though. If you exercise too close to bedtime, you might be too energized to fall asleep. If this seems to be an issue for you, exercise earlier in the day.

7.  **Manage stress.**

## PRIMARY AND SECONDARY INSOMNIA

Insomnia can be *secondary,* a side effect of something else, or *primary. Primary* insomnia is not directly associated with another health condition or problem. When an individual is having difficulty sleeping because of a medical or environmental condition (physical pain, heartburn, depression, medicines, uncomfortable surroundings, or other factor) it is called *secondary* insomnia.[8]

Other conditions linked to insomnia include emotional and mental health problems, metabolic changes, and obesity. Some psychological issues can *contribute* to insomnia such as post-traumatic stress injury (PTSI), mood disorders, and bipolar disorder.[9]

## WARRING AGAINST A SPIRIT OF INSOMNIA

### Lesson One: Remove Negative Emotions

After the first few times I had a spirit of insomnia interfere with sleep, I noticed mild anxiety in the evening whenever we had an early morning meeting scheduled for the following day. Before going to bed, I learned to take a moment, drop down to my spirit, and make sure I had peace. If not, I received forgiveness for harboring any toxic emotion. God didn't give us fear, so we should refuse to give it place in our heart!

> *God has not given us a spirit of fear, but of power and of love and of a sound mind* (2 Timothy 1:7).

Occasionally I would fall asleep easily but be awakened during the night and feel frustrated. Frustration is a form of anger, so I received forgiveness for feeling even a little bit of anger and released myself into God's hands until I felt peace. Then I could fall back asleep.

## Practice

Pray. Close your eyes and get in an attitude of prayer.

Feel. Allow yourself to feel any negative emotion associated with sleep.

Forgive. Receive forgiveness for letting fear influence you.

NOTE: Repeat the process if you wake up during the night and feel fear or frustration.

### Lesson Two: Deal with Generational Insomnia

After the same kind of attack occurred on numerous occasions, I asked Dennis to pray with me because I remembered hearing my late mother tell me she had trouble with insomnia. As soon as I recalled this conversation in prayer, a spirit manifested and Dennis saw an image of my mother's face flash across mine. I forgave my mother and allowed forgiveness to flow back through my family line. Next, I received forgiveness for giving in to the thought, "I hope that doesn't happen to me." That thought alone gave a spirit of insomnia permission to torment me!

## Practice: Generational Insomnia

If a spirit of insomnia runs in your family line and you believe you may have given in to it, you don't have to guess.

Pray. Close your eyes and get in an attitude of prayer.

First. Ask the Lord to show you where it got started in your life—the first person or situation that comes to mind.

Feel. When you see a person or situation, momentarily feel the attached emotion.

Forgive. Receive forgiveness for taking in something God didn't give you. Allow a river of forgiveness to flow from Christ within to the person or release the situation into God's hands. Then release forgiveness back through your family line to ancestors who opened up to that spirit.

### Lesson Three: Understand the Power of Prayer

There is one thing we can absolutely guarantee—the devil doesn't want you to pray. If your sleep is being attacked by a spirit of insomnia, these two strategies may prove to be very effective. After taking common sense steps for good sleep hygiene, prayer could be your answer.

**Pray in the Spirit.** Start praying in the Spirit. Praying in the Spirit helps us to avoid actively engaging our mind, so it is more relaxing mentally. Make this a practice when your sleep is interrupted, and chances are the attacks on your sleep will decrease and eventually stop.

**Get lost in the presence of God.** Stay in bed but get lost in the presence of God. Dropping down to my spirit and yielding to God when I'm in bed, before going to sleep or when I awake in the morning, is a common practice of mine. One night, in spite of everything, sleep evaded me. I stayed in bed but yielded to God, becoming lost in His presence for what seemed like the entire night. In the morning, I discovered that I felt wonderful. No brain fog or physical tiredness!

What could account for this? I knew that deep prayer has a number of effects on us, spirit, soul, and body. Then I ran across some neuroscientific research that gave me an answer! It seems that the role of sleep for optimal brain function was not fully understood until researchers discovered a previously unknown, powerful cleansing mechanism in the brain.

## "BRAIN WASHING"

To understand how prayer could be so refreshing and prevent the aftereffects of insomnia, it helps to know a little about the biology of our brain and the benefit of sleep.

Cellular waste in our body is filtered out by our lymphatic system.[10] Until recently it was believed that the brain didn't have a lymphatic system like the one in the rest of our body and waste products were washed away by the cerebrospinal fluid continually bathing the brain cells (neurons). In 2012, however, neuroscientists discovered another cleansing mechanism that operates during periods of deep sleep.[11]

Scientists named it the *glymphatic* system because it is a separate lymphatic system that relies on *glial* cells[12] in the brain for waste removal. It is a high-pressure hydraulic cleansing system that carries waste away much more forcefully.[13]

> "It's as if the brain has two garbage haulers—a slow one
> that we've known about, and a fast one that we've just
> met," said [Dr. Maiken] Nedergaard.[14]

What happens in our brain when it is being "pressure washed"? The brain cells actually "shrink up" during deep sleep. Space between cells increases by 60 percent and fluid quickly washes through the brain aided by the pulse of the arteries carrying the waste to the liver.[15]

When our brain does not have the opportunity to dispose of waste, it carries the "garbage" from the previous day into the next, and we suffer for it. One reason we feel miserable when we lose sleep is because our brain is still full of "trash" left over from yesterday.

## DEEP PRAYER AND BRAIN WAVES

It has been discovered that brain waves for those in *deep prayer* correspond to the theta and even the delta waves of deep sleep.[16] Therefore, it is possible for us to experience brain cleansing when we are lost in the presence of God. This is the answer I was looking for! We can counteract the effects of insomnia by prayer.

## DAILY EMOTIONAL HYGIENE

Because unresolved emotional issues such as worry or anger can cause difficulty sleeping, we recommend that you spend a short time in prayer before going to bed and let the Lord reveal them. Pray them through one at a time until you get peace. *"Do not let the sun go down on your wrath"* (Eph. 4:26).

Not only can emotional turmoil interfere with sleep directly, our memories are stored as feeling-thought bundles while we are asleep. During the day, our brain continually processes events, impressions, and sensory stimuli as well as retrieving memories into conscious thought as they are triggered. During sleep, however, new information is consolidated and hardwired into the brain.[17]

## HELPING OTHERS

Jesus has already given us authority over the enemy, but we become stronger when we put what the Bible says into practice. *"Solid food belongs to those who are of full age, that is, those who by reason of use have their senses exercised to discern both good and evil"* (Heb. 5:14).

After gaining spiritual strength and becoming determined to win the battle once and for all, I wanted to share what I had learned and help others. Every victory we have increases our spiritual strength and authority so our skirmishes with the enemy become useful.

What better way to exact revenge on the enemy than to help others find freedom?

> *Behold, I give you the authority to trample on serpents and scorpions, and over all the power of the enemy, and nothing shall by any means hurt you* (Luke 10:19).

### Good Sleep Checklist
#### Don't Do This

\_\_\_ Go to bed hungry or stuffed

___ Use electronic devices such as a computer right before bed

___ Take daytime naps

___ Other _____

___ Other _____

### Do This

___ Go to bed and get up at the same time every day

___ Create a bedtime ritual

___ Pray through unresolved emotional issues of the day

___ Engage in relaxing activities (reading, listening to music)

___ Pay attention to what and how much you eat

___ Limit how much you drink before bed

___ Create a room that's ideal for sleeping

- Room-darkening shades
- Earplugs or sound device
- Comfortable mattress and pillow
- Cool room

___ Include regular physical activity in your day

___ Manage stress by staying in peace through forgiveness and release

___ Other _____

___ Other _____

## NOTES

1.    Centers for Disease Control and Prevention (CDC), "Sleep and sleep disorders," *National Center for Chronic Disease Prevention and Health Promotion, Division of Population Health* (March 12, 2015). Retrieved February 25, 2016 from http://www.cdc.gov/sleep/index.html.

2.    A. Ambrogetti, *How to Treat Chronic Insomnia: A Self-Help Manual, Sleep Medicine* (2015). Retrieved February 21, 2016 from http://www.sleepmedicine.com.au/wp-content/uploads/Chronic-Insomnia-A-Self-Help-Manual.pdf.

3.    R. Rosenberg, *Sleep Soundly every Night, Feel Fantastic every Day: A Doctor's Guide to Solving Your Sleep Problems,* (New York, NY: Demos Medical Publishing, LLC, 2014), xviii.

4.    National Institutes of Health, "What is Insomnia?" December 13, 2011, http://www.nhlbi.nih.gov/health/health-topics/topics/inso.

5.    "Why is sleep important?" *National Institutes of Health* (February 22, 2012). Retrieved February 29, 2016 from http://www.nhlbi.nih.gov/health/health-topics/topics/sdd/why.

6.    Healthline Editorial Team (medically reviewed by K.R. Hirsch), "Insomnia complications," *Healthline*, October 13, 2014. Retrieved February 25, 2016 from http://www .healthline.com/health/insomnia-complications#Psychiatrics5.

7.    Mayo Clinic Staff, "Sleep tips: 7 steps to better sleep," *Mayo Clinic In-Depth*, Healthy Lifestyle Adult Health, June 9, 2014. Retrieved February 26, 2016 from http://www .mayoclinic.org/healthy-lifestyle/adult-health/in-depth/sleep/art-20048379.

8.    National Center of Sleep Disorders Research, "Insomnia," Retrieved February 16, 2016 from http://www.amhc .org/100-sleep-disorders/article/7897-insomnia.

9.    Healthline Editorial Team, "Insomnia Complications."

10.   The lymphatic system, part of our immune system, serves as a drainage and filtering system that helps our body get rid of excess fluid and filters out infectious agents, toxins, and waste products. It consists of organs, ducts, and nodes and transports a watery clear fluid which is called lymph. Lymph fluid distributes immune cells throughout the body and also interacts with the blood circulatory system by draining fluid from cells and tissues. The organs of the lymphatic system include bone marrow, lymph nodes, spleen, and thymus.

11.   Like all cells of our body, the neurons in our brain need food and oxygen for metabolism. Cell metabolism produces waste in all cells, including brain cells. During the day, most debris simply collects. The full cleansing of our brain happens while we are in deep sleep via the glymphatic system. Quality sleep is vital to the removal of waste and toxic substances from the brain.

12. Glial cells form a supportive function for the neurons in the brain and the rest of the central nervous system (CNS) and are the most abundant type of cell. Glial cells don't conduct electrical impulses but surround neurons to support, cleanse, and insulate. Without glia, the neurons would not work properly! There are several ways in which glia cells differ from neurons. Neurons have two "processes," but glial cells have only one. Neurons can generate action, but glial cells can't. Unlike neurons, glial cells are not active at all times so they have the potential to rest. Also, neurons have synapses for neurotransmitters, but glial cells don't have chemical synapses. Types and functions of glial cells include:

    - Astrocytes are star-shaped cells that clean up brain wastes, transport nutrients to neurons, hold neurons in place, digest parts of dead neural cells, and regulate content of extracellular space.
    - Microglia also clean the brain by digesting parts of dead neurons.
    - Oligodendroglia provide insulation (myelin) for neurons.
    - Satellite cells provide physical support for neurons in the peripheral nervous system (PNS).
    - Schwann cells provide the insulation (myelin) to neurons in the peripheral nervous system.

13. J.J. Iliff, M. Wang1, Y. Liao B.A. Plogg, W. Peng1, G.A. Gundersen, H. Benveniste, G.E. Vates, R. Deane, S.A. Goldman, E.A. Nagelhus, and M. Nedergaard, "A Paravascular Pathway Facilitates CSF Flow Through the Brain Parenchyma and the Clearance of Interstitial Solutes, Including Amyloid β," *Science Translational Medicine*, August 15,2012: Vol. 4, Issue 147. 147 0.1126/scitranslmed.3003748.

14. "Scientists discover previously unknown cleansing system in brain," Kurzweil Accelerating intelligence (August 16, 2012). Retrieved February 26, 2016 from http://www.kurzweilai.net/scientists-discover-previously-unknown-cleansing-system-in-brain.

15. K. Sinclair, "The glymphatic system – how insomnia leads to a filthy mind," Natural News, December 3, 2014. Retrieved March 8, 2015

from http://www.naturalnews.com/047857 _glymphatic_system_ brain_cells_interstitial_fluid.html.

16. W.C. Dement and C. Vaughn, *The Promise of Sleep: A Pioneer in Sleep Medicine Explores the Vital Connection between Health, Happiness, and a Good Night's Sleep,* (New York, NY: Dell Publishing, a division of Random House, Inc., 1999). 17-26; A. Newberg, E. d'Aquili, and V. Rause, *Why God Won't Go Away: Brain Science and the Biology of Belief,* (New York, NY: Ballantine Books, Random House Publishing Group, 2001), 35-53.

Humans are spirit beings who have souls (thoughts, will, and emotions) and live in bodies. (Animals consist of only soul and body.) God has given us the capacity to interact with the realm of the spirit and discover Him. When we are born again, our spirit is made alive unto God and can then touch God's Spirit. Unsaved individuals also have spirits, but their spirits are "dead," or separated from God.

Both believer and nonbeliever can have spiritual experiences. The question is, what spiritual realm is contacted: evil or Holy. For those seeking deep spiritual experience, or "transcendent states," there is a primary difference between *how* they seek and *what* they seek. Scientists have studied both Christians and non-Christians, people of all types of religious persuasions, and found the neural evidence of spiritual experience is very similar (when studied on brain scans). It should not be surprising that our spiritual capacity can be used both for good and evil. However, when we come to God, we come in faith believing that we can safely open our heart to Him.

> *If a son asks for bread from any father among you, will he give him a stone? Or if he asks for a fish, will he give him a serpent instead of a fish? Or if he asks for an egg, will he offer him a scorpion? If you then, being evil, know how to give good gifts to your children, how much more will your heavenly Father give the Holy Spirit to those who ask Him!* (Luke 11:11–13)

The Christian approach is an active seeking with the intention to quiet the soul (carnal mind, will, and emotions), transcend self, and focus intently on a personal God. Thoughts, emotions, and perceptions are brought under the control of the Holy Spirit and yielded to the Lord. The goal is drawing closer to God. Self is not obliterated but cedes authority to God.

Practitioners of other religions, including new age and eastern mysticism, seek a state of pure awareness, or consciousness of "everything" as an undifferentiated whole through passive seeking. They attempt to clear, or blank out, thoughts, emotions, and perceptions to merge with "everything" and obliterate self. They do not seek a deity who is "out there" and separate from humankind. They believe that the entire universe is part of a cosmic consciousness, or force, with which everything can merge, and become "no-thing," much like pureed vegetable soup.

17.  B. Rasch and J. Born, "About Sleep's Role in Memory," *Physiological Review*, 2013 April; 93(2): 681–766.

To form and retrieve memories is a fundamental ability of any living organism, enabling it to adapt its behavior to the demands of an ever-changing environment, and allowing it to appropriately select and improve the behaviors of a given repertoire. Memory functions comprise three major subprocesses, i.e., encoding, consolidation, and retrieval.

During encoding, the perception of a stimulus results in the formation of a new memory trace, which is initially highly susceptible to disturbing influences and decay, i.e., forgetting.

During consolidation, the labile memory trace is gradually stabilized possibly involving multiple waves of short and long-term consolidation processes...which serve to strengthen and integrate the memory into preexisting knowledge networks.

During retrieval, the stored memory is accessed and recalled....

We assume that whereas the waking brain is optimized for the acute processing of external stimuli that involves the encoding of new information and memory retrieval, the sleeping brain provides optimal conditions for consolidation processes that integrate newly encoded memory into a long-term store. Encoding and consolidation might be mutually exclusive processes inasmuch they draw on overlapping neuronal resources. Thus sleep as a state of greatly reduced external information processing represents an optimal time window for consolidating memories.

*Chapter 13*

# SPIRIT OF LONELINESS

BY DR. JEN,
adapted from
*Simple Keys to Heal Loneliness* eBook.

We have all heard sad stories like this one about a lonely old man in Lyons, France—living and dying in the land of loneliness. A woman who lived in his apartment building writes:

> I knew an old man who lived in the same apartment building as me. ...He had no money and he had no friends and he had no family, and he had no food. ...Every night he would go down to the rubbish bins and try to find something to eat in our rubbish. Every night, we could hear him ripping open the plastic bags and opening and closing the rubbish bins and talking to himself. ...He was completely alone in the world.
>
> No one tried to knock on his door when he first went missing. No one thought about why he suddenly disappeared and no one thought to question why. No one had

seen a removal van or people to help him move. ...No one. He just died, alone, poor, and hungry, without anyone in the world knowing, in his kitchen, with people above and below and on either side of him.[1]

After nine months of missing rent payments, the landlord opened the man's door and found him dead in the kitchen. It seems he had died some seven months earlier.

When we hear about heart-wrenching accounts like this, we become poignantly aware of those who drift to the fringe of society. No family. No friends. No ties to human society. We may momentarily reflect upon the pathos of it all, but quickly forget and go on about our own busy lives.

Are such loneliness and isolation rare? Unfortunately not. While we may not personally relate to the extreme isolation of the lonely old man in Lyons, at least 60 million individuals, one out of every five, in the United States alone suffer from isolation and loneliness that is serious enough to cause persistent unhappiness.[2] Loneliness has become an epidemic in modern society.

## CREATED FOR CONNECTION

We don't have to be *separated* from others to feel lonely. Loneliness and isolation begin in the heart long before the sufferer withdraws from human society. According to research, many individuals report feelings of loneliness even when they do have spouses, family, and friends. For many, isolation is emotional and relational even when they are not physically isolated.

In the Garden of Eden, after God created Adam God told him, *"It is not good that man should be alone"* and brought him a wife (Gen. 2:18). We are made for connection. We need community. Dr. John Cacioppo, one of the founders of social neuroscience, has documented how deeply isolation and loneliness impact our emotional and physical wellbeing. His research shows that social isolation profoundly affects our emotional and physical wellbeing as well as negatively affecting our behavior. Apparently, we cannot overestimate the importance of social connection in human life.

It appears, however, that what matters is not quantity but *quality*—not the number of social connections but "the degree to which social interactions satisfied the individual's specific, subjective need for connection."[3] "What [predicted] loneliness was...an issue of quality: the individuals' ratings of the meaningfulness, or the meaninglessness, of their encounters with other people."[4]

Social connection defines humanity. Human beings were not meant to live in isolation. Emotional connections bond parents and infants together. The emotional information transmitted by parents stabilizes, regulates, and maintains both the physical and emotional health of the infant. This information balances hormone levels, heart function, sleep rhythms, and functioning of the immune system.

As a matter of fact, humans benefit from staying in sync with others throughout their lives for both biological homeostasis as well as companionship. Human society and physiology are interdependent rather than independent.

In a fascinating study of human synchronization,[5] researchers of the Sahlgrenska Academy at the University of Gothenburg in Sweden studied the heart rates of high school choir members as they sang together. Their findings show that singing in unison has soothing effects on the heart. They measured the heart rates of the singers and, when they began to sing together, their heart rates slowed and became synchronized in no time at all.

If singing in unison can have such a dramatic effect on human physiology, how much more can "living in unison" with those we care about stabilize us physiologically?

*Social connection defines humanity.*

If social connection is stabilizing, social isolation destabilizes our perceptions, our behavior, and our health for the worse. Researchers have found that people with few social connections have a greater risk of death from ischemic heart disease, cerebrovascular incidents, circulatory disease and cancer, as well as respiratory, gastrointestinal, and all other factors leading to death.[6] Loneliness and isolation are as much a factor in disease and premature death as high blood pressure, smoking, lack of exercise, or obesity.[7]

## THE GOD CONNECTION

We are not only created for human society, we are made to need God. His design for mankind has always included connection with Him. The Lord has placed within each of us a capacity to discover Him. Throughout the ages, in almost all societies primitive or modern, people have reflected upon the existence of God and the realm of the spirit. There has never been a major civilization that did not embrace some kind of religion.[8] In America, approximately 90 percent of the population believe there is a God. Around the globe, 80 percent of people identify with a religious group.[9]

Is there something in the way we are wired physiologically that causes us to seek God? Are we created to believe? Recent discoveries in neuroscience indicate that humans are made with an inherent capacity for spiritual experience. God encounters are scientifically and measurably real, according to Dr. Andrew Newberg. Newberg says in his book, *How God Won't Go Away*:

> [Science] has surprised us, and our research has left us no choice but to conclude that [those who believe] may be on to something, that the mind's [and heart's] machinery of transcendence may in fact be a window through which we can glimpse the ultimate realness of something that is truly divine.[10]

Studies indicate that those who attend church regularly and engage in religious practices such as having a regular prayer life, enjoying fellowship with other believers, and engaging in charitable activities have better physical, mental, and emotional health[11] than the non-religious or those who rarely or never go to church.

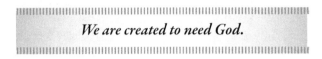

*We are created to need God.*

## LONELINESS IS A SPIRITUAL CONDITION

As it turns out, loneliness is *spiritual* rather than an emotional condition alone. The emotion of sadness precedes the feeling of vacuity. Sadness opens the door of the heart to a spirit of loneliness. Loneliness is experienced as a sense of internal emptiness, or a void, and societal isolation. Individuals who are lonely have a spiritual "shell" around them. Others can perceive the shell and instinctively avoid them.

Many years ago, when I (Dennis) was a new believer, the Lord taught me a significant lesson about loneliness and how He works to heal it. Prior to salvation, I had alternated between self-comforting and exploiting my loneliness. At times, I would turn to entertainment, such as movies, and indulgent eating to ease my discomfort. When I wallowed in self-pity, I would listen to sad music to deliberately stir up the feeling of loneliness invoking self-sympathy—taking on the role of a victim.

One dark evening, leaving the home of relatives, I stopped on the sidewalk outside. Pausing, I gazed up at the street light, which was dimly glowing with a blue hazy light. The light seemed cold and empty, and I felt the loneliness in my gut like an empty ache inside me. Suddenly I realized that not only is God omnipresent, but I was God indwelt because I had asked Jesus into my heart. There could be no place in me that was a "void." He is always with me, so it was impossible to be alone.

Of course, the *emotion* of sadness accompanies loneliness. However, I had felt sadness upon occasion that did not include a feeling of emptiness. At that moment I had a revelation that loneliness was a *spirit of loneliness*, not just emotion. Sadness is an emotion, but loneliness is a spirit. When I received forgiveness for taking in something that God didn't give me, the sense of emptiness and melancholy left and I felt the presence of God filling me.

> *Sadness is an emotion.*
> *Loneliness is a spirit.*

## LONELINESS IS CONTAGIOUS

Research indicates that loneliness appears to be contagious like the flu. It seems to spread in social networks of friends rather than among family members, and female friends are more susceptible than men. Husbands and wives are less likely to "catch" loneliness from each other than from friends. Just one lonely person in your "group" increases your own chances of becoming lonely by 52 percent.[12] Lonely individuals tend to transmit their loneliness to others in their circle of friends, spreading it like an infectious disease.

Secular scientists have discovered there is a *contagion factor* to loneliness, and it can infect others. This phenomenon is not so surprising when we recognize that collective emotional moods and climates are not uncommon. A crowd can become a lynch mob, the joy of a family event such as a wedding can impact relatives and guests alike, and an entire nation may mourn as was the case following 9/11 and the destruction of the Twin Towers.

Loneliness makes individuals less trusting, which increases their difficulty in forming friendships in the first place. When friends become lonely they tend to drift apart rather than maintaining the friendship.

Over time the isolation increases, leading the lonely to gradually drift to the outskirts of society. The non-lonely seem to instinctively pass them by. According to Cacioppo, society rejects the lonely.[13] Loneliness also alters behavior perpetuating and increasing isolation. Loneliness creates an emotional-behavioral cycle that reinforces social anxiety, fear, and other negative feelings. "Others may start to view us less favorably because of our self-protective, sometimes distant, sometimes caustic behavior. This, in turn, merely reinforces our pessimistic social expectations."[14]

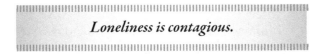

*Loneliness is contagious.*

## LONELINESS-DEPRESSION FEEDBACK LOOP

Loneliness and depression are often paired,[15] according to researchers, although loneliness and depression are clearly distinct conditions.[16] "Loneliness reflects how you feel about your relationships. Depression reflects how you feel period."[17] However, individuals often become trapped in a loneliness-depression feedback loop in which loneliness predicts depression and depression predicts loneliness. Loneliness has within it the desire for companionship mixed with feelings of apprehension and dread. Desire pulls, but fear pushes away.

When individuals are lonely, they become more critical, demanding, and passive. They resist the very relationships they want, and their inner frustration combined with apprehension and passivity give rise to depression. In like manner, depressed individuals often isolate themselves and become lonely.

*Sadness opens the door to loneliness.*

## LONELINESS AND PHYSICAL HEALTH

Loneliness is emotionally painful, but it has physical consequences as well. According to scientific research, loneliness contributes to poor health and increased likelihood of premature death as much as smoking, obesity, and high blood pressure.[18] Chronic feelings of loneliness create a physiological snowball effect that accelerates physical deterioration regardless of age. Loneliness disrupts "key cellular processes deep within the human body. Studies suggest that long-term loneliness is as much a health risk as smoking, obesity or lack of exercise."[19]

> Loneliness...shows up in measurements of stress hormones, immune function, and cardiovascular function. Over time, these changes in physiology are compounded in ways that may be hastening millions of people to an early grave.[20]

Numerous mental and physical diseases that can shorten life are closely correlated with loneliness.[21] Chronic loneliness also makes us susceptible to premature aging.[22] The lonely drink more, eat more, exercise less, get divorced more often, have more family estrangements and run-ins with neighbors, and their general health declines more with age when compared to the non-lonely.[23]

*Loneliness can make you*
*sick, older, and dead.*

## LONELINESS IS A PERCEPTION

Those who are struggling with loneliness may not actually *be* alone, but they feel very, very alone. Loneliness has been described as *perceived* social isolation, and it is not correlated with the actual number of people in a person's life. Lonely people often say they constantly feel as though they "don't belong" or "don't fit in." Many have lost hope and have "shut down" emotionally. Many are bitter about their "lot in life" underneath the sadness.

Connection is the answer for life satisfaction and emotional health. What matters is the degree to which social interactions satisfy individuals' needs. People can be lonely in a crowd. Other individuals, such as artists or writers can be quite content to spend long hours alone. What predicts loneliness is the quality of relationships—how meaningful or meaningless their encounters are with people.[24]

The best demographic predictor of loneliness is marriage, but Cacioppo stresses it's a very loose predictor.[25] A spouse in an unhappy marriage can be as just as lonely as a single person, and perhaps even more so. It can actually be easier to live alone than endure rejection within your own household. Fortunately, individuals can have fulfilling social connections in ways other than marriage. Friends substitute quite well for relatives or a spouse in providing meaningful social bonds.

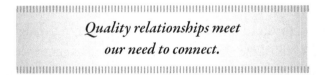

*Quality relationships meet*
*our need to connect.*

## HEALING LONELINESS

Robert went from church to church but never felt like he "fit in." He says, "Usually the loneliness would grab hold of me and I would isolate myself. There was less chance of being hurt, I told myself, fewer opportunities for being rejected. Consequently, after being at a church for a few years, I would leave totally disillusioned." After Robert read one of my articles on loneliness, which included steps for healing, he prayed on his own.

> I knew "loneliness" was an issue for me. So I asked the Lord to reveal to me how this came into my life. Immediately in my mind's eye He took me back to my birthday when I was about six or seven years old. I was at home sick. It was a dreary November day, cold and rainy. I was holding my new toy and looking out the picture window and feeling very lonely. After seeing this scene...I dropped down in prayer focusing on my belly to where Christ dwells.
>
> As I was feeling this loneliness, I asked Jesus to go to that feeling and move right through it. He did and peace came to me. I asked the Lord to reveal His truth to me. ...The Lord confirmed what He had done later that evening. I went to "home group" that was part of the church that I have been attending for the last year. What was interesting is that I had been feeling isolated in this group over the last few weeks.
>
> That night the feeling of isolation was gone. ...While we were praying for one another at the end of the meeting the joy of the Lord rose up in my belly and I began to laugh. ... He so filled me with His Spirit that I had to get up slowly and had to sit for a while before I could drive home. ...As I write this, His presence is so wonderful and it is nice to know deep down inside that I don't feel weird anymore. I feel that I am unique and specially made by the Lord Himself. That is so amazing because I know that feeling is available to every one of His children.

## SIMPLE KEYS FOR HEALING LONELINESS

Sadness is the open door that allows loneliness to come in. After closing that emotional door, we then welcome the presence of God to fill the void.

| Practice: Healing Loneliness |
|---|
| **Pray.** Close your eyes and pray. |
| **First.** In an attitude of prayer, picture the first person or situation that comes to mind. |
| **Feel.** Feel the feeling. Let yourself feel any sadness or loneliness momentarily. |
| **Forgive.** Receive forgiveness from Christ in you until it changes to peace. |
| **Fill.** Welcome the presence of God into that area. Let Him fill any emptiness in you. |

## SEVEN PRACTICAL STEPS

Here are seven additional steps to take:

1. **Resist the spirit of loneliness.** Don't give it ground again. God is with you always to strengthen you.

   *Be of good courage, and He shall strengthen your heart, all you who hope in the Lord* (Psalm 31:24).

2. **Pursue a relationship with God.** God wants His people to put Him first. Seek Him and He will be with you!

   *The Lord will command His lovingkindness in the daytime, and in the night His song shall be with me—a prayer to the God of my life* (Psalm 42:8).

   *For He Himself has said, "I will never leave you nor forsake you"* (Hebrews 13:5b).

3. **Find a church home** if you don't already have one. Ask God to show you where He wants you to connect with a church family.

   *God sets the solitary in families* (Psalm 68:6).

4. **Reach out to others in small ways.** Find safe places to experiment with making social signals—eye contact, smiling, or making small talk. Just the simple act of acknowledging another human being helps shift your focus from yourself...and you have made a small connection that is real. (Do not expect everyone to reciprocate positively, although the vast majority will do so. Remember that some individuals might have just received bad news, feel physically ill, or have their own private pain.)

5. **Ask God to send you friends.** Matthew 6:33 says, *"Seek first the kingdom of God and His righteousness and all these* [other] *things will added to you."* That includes proper relationships.

6. **Be patient and take small steps.** You are learning a new way to live.

7. **For additional help**, we have other resources available at www.forgive123.com.

### NOTES

1.  Fripouille, "The story of the old and lonely man," (2009). (October 28, 2010) http://www.nowpublic.com/health/story-old-and-lonely-man.

2.  D.E. Steffick, "Documentation on affective functioning measures in the Health and Retirement Study," Documentation Report no. DR-005 (Ann Arbor,MI: University of Michigan, Survey Research Center, 2000). (May 19, 2010) www.hrsonline.isr.umich.edu/docs/

userg/dr-005
.pdf.

3.   J. Cacioppo and W. Patrick. *Loneliness: Human Nature and the Need for Social Connection.* (W.W. Norton & Company: New York, NY, 2008), 94.

4.   L. Wheeler, H. Reis, and J.B. Nezlek, "Loneliness, social interaction, and sex roles," Journal of Personality and Social Psychology 45 (1983): 943-953. L.C. Hawkley, M.H. Burleson, B.B. Berntson, and J.T. Cacioppo, "Loneliness in everyday life: Cardiovascular activity, psychosocial context, and health behaviors," *Journal of Personality and Social Psychology* 85 (2003): 105-120.

5.   B. Vickhoff, H. Malmgren, R. Åström, G. Nyberg, S. Ekström, M. Engwall, J. Snygg, M. Nilsson, and R. Jörnsten, "Music structure determines heart rate variability of singers," *Frontiers of Psychology*, (July 9, 2013). (October 4, 2013) http://www.frontiersin.org/ Auditory_Cognitive _Neuroscience/10.3389/fpsyg.2013.00334/ abstract

6.   L.F. Berkman and S.L. Syme, "Social networks, host resistance and mortality: A nine-year follow-up study of Alameda County residents," *American Journal of Epidemiology* 109, no. 2 (1979): 186-204.

7.   J.S. House, K.R. Landis, and D. Umbertson, "Social relationships and health," Science 241 (1988): 540-545.

8.   "More than 9 in 10 Americans continue to believe in God," Gallup Poll (June 3, 2011). Retrieved September 8, 2013 from http://www. gallup.com/poll/147887/Americans-Continue -Believe-God.aspx.

9.   "The global religious landscape," Pew Research Center, Religion and Public Life (December 18, 2012). Retrieved September 8, 2013 from http://www.pewforum.org.

10.   A. Newberg, *How God Won't Go Away* (New York, NY: The Random House Publishing Group, 2001), 140.

11.   H.G. Koenig, *The Healing Power of Faith* (New York, NY: Simon and Schuster, 2001), 258; J.S. Levin, "Religion and health: Is there an association, is it valid, and is it causal?" Social Science Medicine 38:1475-1482, 1994.

12. J.T. Cacioppo, J.H. Fowler, and N.A. Christakis, "Alone in the crowd: the structure and spread of loneliness in a large social network." *Journal of Personality and Social Psychology* 97(6) (2009 December): 977–991.

13. Ibid.

14. J. Cacioppo and W. Patrick, *Loneliness: Human Nature and the Need for Social Connection.* (New York, NY: W.W. Norton & Company, 2008), 34.

15. C. Segrin, "Interpersonal communication problems associated with depression and loneliness," in P.A. Andersen and L.K. Guerrero, eds., Handbook of communication and emotion: Research theory, applications, and contexts (San Diego, CA: Academic Press, 1998): 215-242.

16. R.S. Weiss, ed., "Loneliness: The experience of emotional and social isolation," (Cambridge, MA: MIT Press, 1973); J.T. Cacioppo, L.C. Hawkley, J.M. Ernst, M. Burleson, G. Berntson, B. Nouriani, and D. Spiegel, "Loneliness with a nomological net: An evolutionary perspective," *Journal of Affective Disorders* 72 (2002): 1-14.

17. Cacioppo, Loneliness: Human Nature, 83.

18. J.S. House, K.R. Landis, and D. Umberson. "Social relationships and health." *Science* 241(4865) (July 29, 1988): 540-5.

19. University of Chicago News, "Loneliness undermines health as well as mental well-being," (September 3, 2008). (April 12, 2010) http://news.uchicago.edu/article/2008/09/03/loneliness-undermines-health-well-mental-well-being

20. Cacioppo, Loneliness: Human Nature, 5.

21. Ibid., 92-109.

22. Ibid., 34.

23. Ibid., 102.

24 Ibid., 94.

25. J.T. Cacioppo, J.H. Fowler, and N.A. Christakis "Alone in the Crowd: The Structure and Spread of Loneliness in a Large Social Network," *Journal of Personality and Social Psychology* 97(6) (December 2009): 977–991; Cacioppo, *Loneliness: Human Nature,* 81.

*Chapter 14*

# SEDUCING SPIRITS, AGENDAS, AND SOULISH PRAYERS

Demons do not hitchhike on all fleshly manifestations, inner wounds, or sin, but sexual sins automatically give legal ground to demons. Seducing spirits are given permission to infest a person's life when sexual sin is committed. They manifest as feelings of arousal, which are similar to the excitement of butterflies in the gut but also feel unclean. This sensation is similar in other areas where lust is involved such as addictions, gossip, gluttony, and so forth, although there may be other more sexually specific impressions as well as shame and guilt. It doesn't matter if there hasn't been actual sexual involvement. Seducing spirits can even link to emotional attachments without physical contact.

The common denominator for soul ties, idols, and agendas is the emotion of lust. A soul tie to the object of lust and a seducing spirit is always present.

> *Sexual sins automatically*
> *give demons legal ground.*

## UNHEALTHY SOUL TIES

Emotional attachments may be good or bad. An unhealthy soul tie is a result of the sin of lust, an impure emotional connection, and always has a seducing spirit attached. Although it may feel titillating, a seducing spirit also feels unclean. On the other hand, healthy emotional connections come from bonds of genuine love or affection that feel clean and pure.

| Healthy Emotional Attachment | Unhealthy Soul Tie |
|---|---|
| Healthy friendship<br>Husband-wife<br>Parent-child<br>Brothers-sisters<br>Extended family<br>Christian bonds of fellowship (see Eph. 4:3) | Sexual violation (rape, sexual molestation)<br>Romantic (possible) or sexual involvement<br>Parent-child (parental inversion or substitute mate<br>Fantasy (pornography, romance novels)<br>Fetish (sexual attraction to a body part or an object)<br>Emotional attachment to former spouse after death or divorce<br>Lust for spouse<br>Obsession with celebrity or political figure<br>Obsession of a stalker |

A soul tie does not disappear over time and can resurface many years later. A person can see a former girlfriend or boyfriend after a span of decades and still experience an instantaneous attraction. Soul ties are not always romantic attachments. Parents can even develop soul ties with their own children. Parental inversion[1] or substitute mate[2] relationships may occur when a parent consciously or unconsciously encourages the child to fulfill the role of a spouse. Also, clients sometimes form soul ties with counselors or physicians and vice versa.

> *Breaking a soul tie removes its pull.*

A pastor I (Dennis) knew had an emotional relationship with a young woman in his youth, but they parted ways in college. He moved away from the area, married, had children, and became a pastor. When the former girlfriend showed up in town 20 years later, he was shocked that a powerful attraction to her was instantly rekindled. He made an appointment with me and prayed through forgiveness and repentance and also broke the soul tie he had with her. The power of the seducing spirit was instantly nullified and that door was closed. We must take back ground from the enemy to successfully resist evil.

In another case, a prominent Christian minister fell into sexual sin, losing his church, ministry, and reputation. Several years later, I saw him on television talking openly about what had happened. He mentioned that he had been molested as a child and had struggled with overwhelming temptation from that time until the present. Although he had, for a time, successfully resisted with willpower, the day came when willpower failed and he committed sexual sin. Willpower is not powerful enough to withstand temptation forever. Flesh cannot guard flesh. Spirit, good or evil, always outlasts flesh.

> *Spirit always outlasts flesh.*

If an individual develops an emotional attraction with someone other than a spouse they are entering into dangerous territory. When a married person forms a close emotional attachment with someone (same or opposite sex) other than their spouse, they may develop an unhealthy soul tie or spiritual adultery. If spiritual adultery is not dealt with, it often escalates to physical adultery.

As soon as emotional bonding or physical desire (passion) begins to be aroused, human spirits form an unholy one-flesh covenant bond, and seducing spirits mold around it. Emotional attachments among co-workers are so common in the business world that the expression "work spouse" has been coined.

> A work spouse is a co-worker of the opposite sex with whom you have a close platonic relationship. In many ways, these relationships can mirror a real marriage. According to a 2007 survey from Vault.com, a career information web site, 23 percent of workers reported that they had a work spouse.[3]

Believers must continue to be vigilant after breaking a soul tie because the other party will often attempt to re-establish the connection.

> *You have heard that it was said to those of old, "You shall not commit adultery." But I say to you that whoever looks at a woman to lust for her has already committed adultery with her in his heart* (Matthew 5:27-28).

> *Whoever commits adultery with a woman lacks understanding; he...destroys his own soul* (Proverbs 6:32).

## IDOLS

A person, place, or thing someone wants so strongly they can't "let it go" becomes an idol. For a believer, it is anything they want more than God. A sure sign idolatry is involved is the inability to be neutral before God about it. We ministered to a young woman once who insisted on having a house at the beach. She moved to a different location and bought a house at the beach without consulting God. When we saw her a few years later, she told us she couldn't find a good church to attend, had made no friends, and that it had been years since she experienced the presence of God.

A certain young woman named Barbara was adamant that she needed a father for her child who had been born out of wedlock. She laid out a "fleece" and a man came into her life who satisfied the fleece (see Judges 6:36–40). The man moved in with her, but he had serious mental problems bordering on psychosis. Ultimately, she lost custody of her child and the relationship with the man ended. Having an idol can cause us to lose the very thing we want most.

> *An idol can cause us to lose*
> *what we want most.*

## AGENDAS

Although agendas are commonplace in all areas of life, they are particularly destructive in the church. It is common for believers to want a ministry position, such as worship leader, and go from church to church looking for a platform for their ministry. The proper heart attitude is to seek God Himself first and attend the church of His choosing, even if there is no apparent possibility of satisfying their ambitions. God is more interested in our character than our gifting.

*Exaltation [promotion] comes neither from the east nor from the west nor from the south. But God is the Judge: He puts down one, and exalts another* (Psalm 75:6-7).

Two lies that Christians often believe are 1) a leader is holding them back, or 2) they have to help God out. The truth is God is more interested in character than gifting. If we let the Lord get our heart right He will open up the opportunity for ministry. Jesus had approximately three years of ministry, but Father God prepared Him as a man for 30 years: *"Though He was a Son, yet He learned obedience by the things which He suffered"* (Heb. 5:8).

> *Character is more important*
> *to God than gifting.*

## Practice: Agendas and Idolatry

You don't have to guess about whether or not you have an agenda or idol. If you ask the Lord to show you an idol, He will be faithful to bring it to mind if you have one. Close your eyes and pray.

**First.** What is the first person, place, or thing that comes to mind?

**Feel.** Feel the feeling in your gut.

NOTE: When a seducing spirit manifests, it feels "tingly" or arousing. You don't have to guess about wrong relationships, idols, or agendas; you can instantly verify it by the feeling it produces.

**Forgive.** Receive forgiveness. (You may need to forgive another person or God if you have been demanding something from Him or are angry at Him.)

**Release.** Release the idol (from the gut) into the hands of God with no strings attached. Let it go until you feel peace.

Your attitude should be, "Even if I never get what I want, I am leaving it up to God to make the decision." When you release an idol you will feel peace in your gut and the "pull" will be gone.

## INNER VOWS

Inner vows are made at the time of emotional wounding and create a willpower wall as a form of self-protection. They are similar to a fear guard in that, regardless of the primary emotion, the individual believes fear can keep them safe. Examples of inner vows include: "No one will ever hurt me again." "I'll never trust another man." "I can't let anyone know how I really feel." "I'll never get fat like my mother." We treat them in much the same way as mental strongholds with an added step to "unlock" the will.

### Practice: Inner Vows

What God says is spiritual truth or fact. Anything that doesn't line up with God's Word or nature comes from the wrong kingdom. He never tells us to protect ourselves with willpower. We put up walls at a time of emotional wounding, so we start with the emotion. When we have peace, we are in the place of authority with power to dislodge the stronghold.

**Pray.** Close your eyes and get in an attitude of prayer.

**First.** What is the first person or situation that comes to mind?

**Feel.** Feel the feeling. Allow yourself to **feel**. What emotion do you feel in your gut when you picture that person or situation? (Every thought has a corresponding emotion.)

**Forgive.** Yield to Christ the forgiver within and allow a river of forgiveness to flow from the belly until the emotion changes to peace. Allow forgiveness to flow out to others if you blame others. If you are angry at or disappointed with God, receive forgiveness for judging Him. If you are upset with yourself, yield and receive forgiveness from Christ within.

### Removing a Willpower Wall

The next step is removal of the wall and welcoming God to take His place as our Protector.

Breaking vows. After applying forgiveness and getting peace, allow yourself to feel the wall or barrier. Yield to Christ within and allow a river of forgiveness to flow through that wall and remove it.

If you are hesitant to remove the wall, that is a reaction of your flesh. The new creation you always agrees with God and His Word. Choose to side with the new creation you. Jesus never gets stuck, and He is able to remove any wall so His peace can be your protection. Allow forgiveness to flow through the wall until you feel peace.

Renounce and **Release.** After forgiving and getting peace, renounce the vow out loud and release yourself into the hands of God.

Welcome God's protection. Welcome the Lord as your Protector.

## HEAVENLY VS. HISTORICAL RECORD

The reality of committing sexual sin or being molested is a matter of historical record. We can't change history, and our memories can't be "erased." However, we can be healed and cleansed. Our head remembers but our heart can be free. When God heals us, we have a testimony—a new heavenly record of peace in our heart, a cleansed conscience, and a story to share with others.[4] When the Lord heals our wounds and traumas, forgiveness washes away negative emotions and replaces them with an anointing of supernatural peace.

## SOULISH PRAYERS

The force of someone's willpower directed toward us can affect us spiritually. We may feel unusual pressure or anxiety in the atmosphere as a result. Even though we may feel peace in our heart, the soulish energy can manifest in physical symptoms such as dizziness. When you feel oppression but have peace inside, release forgiveness to anyone who might be praying against the will of God for your life. If you accidently give in so you take in a negative atmosphere, receive forgiveness and you will get your peace back.

Believers can also get headaches, backaches, or other physical pains that are caused by spiritual pressure rather than a physical condition. If this is the case, release forgiveness toward the unknown person(s) responsible, receive forgiveness for taking in something God didn't give you, and rebuke demonic activity. We must remember, also, that people aren't the enemy. They are just used by the enemy.

> *We do not wrestle against flesh and blood, but against principalities, against powers, against the rulers of the darkness of this age, against spiritual hosts of wickedness in the heavenly places* (Ephesians 6:12).

## Practice: Dealing with Soulish Prayers

If you feel pressure in the atmosphere or a suspicious headache, first make sure you have peace inside.

Pray: Drop down and get in an attitude of prayer.

**Forgive.** Release forgiveness to whomever is responsible. You don't have to know the source of the pressure, just generally forgive those who are responsible.

Receive. If you still have a headache, receive forgiveness for taking in something God didn't give you.

Renounce and Rebuke. If you feel it's necessary, one more step may be advisable. Speaking aloud, renounce control, soulish prayers, all curses, and command evil spirits to go.

## SEDUCING SPIRITS

When an individual has a seducing spirit, it is common for them to lose their ability to make logical decisions, listen to reason, understand the Bible correctly, or apply biblical principles. Although they may have been rational prior to engaging in sin, the presence of the demonic activity seems to give some believers what we call "the stupids," for lack of a better term.

> *The path of the just is like the shining sun that shines ever brighter unto the perfect day. The way of the wicked is like darkness; they do not know what makes them stumble* (Proverbs 4:18-19).

*His own iniquities entrap the wicked man, and he is caught in the cords of his sin. He shall die for lack of instruction, and in the greatness of his folly he shall go astray* (Proverbs 5:22-23).

Individuals also get "the stupids" when they have idols in the heart, agendas, or fantasy outcomes created with their own imagination. Idols skew our perception so we see and hear through a demonic filter. Sometimes believers with an idol may use religious sounding (but not truly godly) reasoning, faith talk, denial, or engage in repetitive rituals.

*Therefore speak to them, and say to them, "Thus says the Lord God: 'Everyone of the house of Israel who sets up his idols in his heart, and puts before him what causes him to stumble into iniquity, and then comes to the prophet, I the Lord will answer him who comes, according to the multitude of his idols'"* (Ezekiel 14:4).

> **Seducing spirits and idols can give you "the stupids."**

### Practice: Dealing with Seducing Spirits

In sexual sin or when we are sinned against, there may be a variety of emotions that surface including arousal, guilt, shame, disgust, fear, and so forth. Sometimes there is anger toward someone who failed to provide protection or toward God if we blame Him. "Why did God allow that to happen to me?" Often a person blames themselves even if they were clearly victimized. Both real and imagined guilt are resolved the same way—by receiving forgiveness.

**Pray.** In an attitude of prayer, pray in order as people or events come to mind.

**Feel the feeling.** Dealing with the titillation or arousal specifically is necessary for dealing with the seducing spirit. If you just feel guilt and shame, deal with that first then allow yourself to feel the arousal.

**Forgive.** Forgive God, self, and others. Receive forgiveness and cleansing. Pray through emotional wounds, such as hurt or fear, as well as titillation or arousal, guilt, and shame. Sometimes different emotions must be prayed through individually.

Receive cleansing. Receive forgiveness and cleansing from Christ within. Allow the Lord to cleanse your spirit. Your head will remember, but your spirit can forget.

Break soul ties. Break soul tie(s) and give your emotions back to God. In the case of pornography, soul ties in fantasy relationships need to be broken. Usually demonic activity leaves automatically, but it can be rebuked if necessary.

## WARFARE STRATEGY

Unhealthy soul ties attract the wrong people, cause us to become involved in unhealthy relationships, and release the purposes of the enemy for destruction (see 1 Pet. 5:8). The Lord desires to break ungodly soul ties and loose us from bondage.

> *The Lord shall go forth like a mighty man; He shall stir up His zeal like a man of war. He shall cry out, yes, shout aloud; He shall prevail against His enemies* (Isaiah 42:13).

> *Shake yourself from the dust; arise...[and] loose yourself from the bonds of your neck, O captive Daughter of Zion* (Isaiah 52:2 AMPC).

When we are free, the Lord can connect us in healthy relationships in the right way (see Eph. 4:3). If we aren't entangled with unhealthy soul ties, God can bring healthy relationships into our life through cooperation with *divine appointments, divine connections, divine order,* and *divine purpose.* The Lord must deliver us from unclean entanglements to accomplish His purposes through us.

*The thief does not come except to steal, and to kill, and to destroy.* **I have come that they may have life, and that they may have it more abundantly** (John 10:10).

## FOUR LEVELS OF COOPERATION

1. A **divine appointment** is an encounter with a key person that has been specifically and unmistakably inspired by God (see Gen. 24:4,48).

2. A **divine connection** is a God-ordained relationship (see Gen. 24:61–67).

3. **Divine order** positions us in the right place, at the right time, with the right people.

   *God places the solitary in families* (Psalm 68:6 AMPC).

   *For I know the thoughts that I think toward you, says the Lord, thoughts of peace and not of evil, to give you a future and a hope* (Jeremiah 29:11).

4. **Divine purpose** establishes God's plan for our life and His purposes on earth. We don't design our own story but enter God's story.

   *But seek first the kingdom of God and His righteousness, and all these things [including proper relationships] shall be added to you* (Matthew 6:33).

   *If Abraham, by what he did for God, got God to approve him, he could certainly have taken credit for it.* **But the story we're given is a God-story, not an Abraham-story.** *What we read in Scripture is, "Abraham entered into what God was doing for him, and that was the turning point. He trusted God to set him right instead of trying to be right on his own"* (Romans 4:1–3 MSG).

## NOTES

1.  Parental inversion occurs when a parent is unable or unwilling to fulfill their role and the child takes on the role of caretaker for the parent. The parentally inverted child will bear the weight of care and responsibility which should rest on the parent. Unhealed parental inversion invariably leads to unhealthy relationships later in life.

2.  Substitute mate is a more serious form of parental inversion in which a parent relies inappropriately on a child of the opposite sex for emotional comfort or, in worst scenarios, for physical satisfaction.

3.  E. Patrick, "Seven signs you have a work spouse," CNN.com/living, November 10, 2008. (June 2, 2010) http://www.cnn.com/2008/LIVING/worklife/11/10/cb.seven.signs.work.spouse.

4.  The historical record reveals the sins of David, but repentance and forgiveness cleanse the heavenly or spiritual record. David committed adultery with Bathsheba and had her husband murdered (see 2 Sam. 11:1–17). However, the Lord says of David, *"I have found David the son of Jesse, a man after My own heart, who will do all My will"* (Acts 13:22). In Psalm 51, a repentant David humbled himself before the Lord and received forgiveness: *"Purge me with hyssop, and I shall be clean; wash me, and I shall be whiter than snow....Create in me a clean heart, O God"* (Ps. 51:7,10).

*Chapter 15*

# HEALING EMOTIONAL FOUNDATIONS

To have an emotionally healthy life, we require adequate foundations in the areas of trust, love, personal value, and purpose. Wounds suffered early in life can interfere with our ability to trust. A failure to trust produces fear. If you have difficulty trusting, however, God knows where that issue began in your life and is more than willing to heal and *fill* deficient areas.

Trust is the foundation of all relationships and our emotional health. It enables us to give and receive love, feel personal worth or value, and find a sense of purpose in life. If our foundation of trust is inadequate, our other foundations cannot form properly.

God gave us these legitimate emotional needs and also made it possible for us to receive what we require from our parents. Emotional needs are *legitimate*. A baby needs food and water, clothing, shelter, and love from parents—both physical and emotional sustenance.

Ideally, parents should give their children good emotional foundations. Emotional wholeness is designed to be generational—a blessing passed from parents to children to grandchildren.

> *Fathers, do not irritate and provoke your children to anger [do not exasperate them to resentment], but rear them [tenderly] in the training and discipline and the counsel and admonition of the Lord* (Ephesians 6:4 AMPC).

> *Our basic human needs are God-given.*

Because parents are often flawed, however, God made provision for both our healing and re-parenting. It doesn't matter what you have been through, God has help for you and is able to provide all you needed but didn't receive. Father God sent His own Son, Jesus, to die for us so we could receive His supernatural love and acceptance and restore faulty foundations.

> *When my father and my mother forsake me, then the Lord will take care of me* (Psalm 27:10).

God also has a plan for a *new* family, the household of faith. It is absolutely correct to talk about your church "home." That is exactly what it is designed to be. Ask the Lord to show you where He wants you go to church.

> *God sets the solitary in families* (Psalm 68:6a).

> *[Jesus] came and preached peace to you who were far away and peace to those who were near. For through him we both have access to the Father by one Spirit. Consequently, you are no longer foreigners and strangers, but fellow citizens with*

*God's people and also members of his household* (Ephesians 2:17–19 NIV).

*And let us consider one another in order to stir up love and good works, not forsaking the assembling of ourselves together, as is the manner of some, but exhorting one another* (Hebrews 10:24-25).

## EMOTIONAL BLACK HOLES

Emotionally bankrupt parents have little emotional support to give to their children. They can't give something they never received themselves. If their own emotional needs are unmet, parents can't meet the emotional needs of their children. Nothing can ever fill a "black hole" in outer space. It just keeps absorbing more and more matter.[1] Unmet needs in childhood result in *emotional black holes*. Individuals try to fill the inner craving with counterfeits that never satisfy.

*You can't give what you never received.*

## FILLING EMOTIONAL NEEDS

When key elements are lacking in childhood, an individual may spend the rest of their life trying to meet their needs. Unfortunately, this pursuit is extremely damaging because people choose unhealthy ways of searching. Emotional neediness pushes other people away and robs us of the very happiness we are seeking. Most social and relational problems come from trying to meet needs in the wrong way.

When individuals try to meet needs with counterfeits, they develop a soul tie with persons, places, or things (idolatry). Such soul ties have seducing spirits attached that cause an emotional "pull," so deliverance is part of healing.

### Practice: Filling a Simple Need

**Pray.** Close your eyes and get in an attitude of prayer.

**First.** Ask the Lord to reveal an area of emotional need.

**Feel:** Feel the emotion momentarily.

**Forgive.** Forgive the person(s) who didn't give you what you needed until you get peace.

**Release.** Release any demands on people and release any substitute(s) or idols.

**Fill.** Then connect to Christ within, the fountain of Living Water, and allow Him to fill you.

In codependent relationships, one or both parties attempt to fulfill their emotional needs through their partner. They often go from one unhealthy relationship to another. Codependent individuals fear being abandoned or rejected and develop relational patterns of control and manipulation.

> Imperfect families often produce children who learn that to get their real needs met (safety, value, acceptance, etc.) they must give up important parts of themselves and conform to parental/societal expectations. The child learns the behaviors that will get these needs met. These behaviors may become patterned into codependency based personality roles.... When a [codependent] child takes on these roles there is an inevitable loss of the authentic self.[2]

It is common for a codependent individual to become a "rescuer" and get a sense of purpose through caretaking. They often alternate between fear of being abandoned and anger because they feel used.

> Codependency is...an emotional and behavioral condition that affects an individual's ability to have a healthy, mutually satisfying relationship. It is also known as "relationship addiction" because people with codependency

often form or maintain relationships that are one-sided, emotionally destructive and/or abusive.

Codependents have low self-esteem and look for anything outside of themselves to make them feel better. They find it hard to "be themselves." Some try to feel better through alcohol, drugs or nicotine—and become addicted. Others may develop compulsive behaviors like workaholism, gambling, or indiscriminate sexual activity....

As this reliance increases, the codependent develops a sense of reward and satisfaction from "being needed." When the caretaking becomes compulsive, the codependent feels...helpless in the relationship, but is unable to break away from the cycle of behavior that causes it. Codependents view themselves as victims and are attracted to that same weakness in the love and friendship relationships.[3]

Because codependency comes from issues in early childhood, it is important to allow God to minister to the roots and fill the emotional holes.

## Practice: Filling an Emotional Hole

**Pray.** Close your eyes and get in an attitude of prayer.

**First:** Focus on the first person or situation that comes to mind.

**Feel:** Feel the emotion momentarily.

**Forgive:** Allow a river of forgiveness to flow.

**Fact:** Forgive, renounce the lie, if any, then ask the Lord for the truth.

**Release:** Release demands on people who didn't give you what you needed.

**Fill.** Finally, welcome the presence of God to fill that area of need.

### Breaking an Unhealthy Soul Tie

**Pray:** In an attitude of prayer, pray in the order people or events come to mind, one at a time.

**First.** Focus on the first person or situation that comes to mind.

**Feel.** Feel the feeling.

**Forgive:** Forgive God, self, and others. Receive forgiveness and cleansing.

Sometimes different emotions must be prayed through individually. For example, there is usually titillation or arousal, guilt, and shame. Dealing with the titillation or arousal specifically is necessary for dealing with the seducing spirit. If you just feel guilt and shame, deal with that first, then allow yourself to feel the arousal momentarily, then both release and receive forgiveness.

**Receive cleansing:** Receive cleansing from Christ within. Allow the Lord to wash and cleanse your spirit. Your head will remember, but God can cause your spirit to forget.

**Receive deliverance from soul ties:** Break a soul tie as an act of your will. Finally, give your emotions back to God. Usually demonic activity leaves automatically, but it can be rebuked if necessary.

## Dealing with Worrisome Thoughts

Individuals suffering from emotional neediness are often tormented by troubling thoughts or impressions such as:

"I must have a relationship to feel worthwhile."

"I have a purpose in life when someone needs me."

"I must have the approval of others to feel good about myself."

"I have to be in control or I won't get what I need."

**Pray.** Close your eyes and get in an attitude of prayer.

**First.** What is the first person or situation that comes to mind?

**Feel.** Feel the feeling. Allow yourself to **feel.** What emotion do you feel in your gut when you picture that person or situation? (Every thought has a corresponding emotion.)

**Forgive.** Yield to Christ the forgiver within and allow a river of forgiveness to flow from the belly until the emotion changes to peace. Allow forgiveness to flow out to others if you blame others. If you are angry at or disappointed with God, receive forgiveness for judging Him. If you are upset with yourself, yield and receive forgiveness from Christ within.

**Renounce.** Renounce the thought. When you have peace, you are in the place of authority.

## *Replacing a Lie with the Truth*

Just because you have had a thought or impression for a long time doesn't mean it's true. The only legitimate standard is God and His Word.

**Pray.** Close your eyes and get in an attitude of prayer.

**First.** What is the first person or situation that comes to mind?

**Feel.** Feel the feeling. Allow yourself to **feel**. What emotion do you feel in your gut when you picture that person or situation? (Every thought has a corresponding emotion.)

**Forgive.** Yield to Christ the forgiver within and allow a river of forgiveness to flow from the belly until the emotion changes to peace.

Fact. Always deal with the emotion first to wash out the negative emotion and replace it with peace. When we forgive and get peace, we are in the place of power with the spiritual authority to dislodge lies and replace them with truth.

Renounce. After forgiving and getting peace, renounce the troubling thought or impression out loud.

Replace. Next, ask the Lord for the truth (scriptural fact) and receive it into your heart. Truth comes from God through our spirit and informs our mind.

NOTE: Lies always come in at the time of emotional wounding, but very few emotional wounds have lies attached. In our experience, in only one out of every 30 or 40 wounds was a lie believed.

## NOTES

1.  "Black holes are some of the strangest and most fascinating objects found in outer space. They are objects of extreme density with such strong gravitational attraction that even light cannot escape from their grasp if it comes near enough." N.T. Redd, "Black Holes: Facts, theory and definition," Space, April 9, 2015. Retrieved March 25, 2016 from http://www .space.com/15421-black-holes-facts-formation-discovery -sdcmp. html#sthash.0GpZslkj.dpuf.

2.  P.B. McGinnis, "Codependency: Abandonment of self," January 9, 2001. Retrieved March 18, 2004 from http://www .dr-mcginnis.com/codependency.htm.

3.  "Co-dependency," Mental Health America. Retrieved September 19, 2015 from http://www.mentalhealthamerica .net/co-dependency.

*Chapter 16*

# Religious Spirits

Religious spirits hitchhike on human willpower. True worship of God comes only from the Holy Spirit. *"God is Spirit, and those who worship Him must worship in spirit and truth"* (John 4:24). When we worship the Lord in spirit and truth, we love God with the love He has given us, not our carnal emotions.

> *We love Him because He first loved us* (1 John 4:19).

> *The love of God has been poured out in our hearts by the Holy Spirit who was given to us* (Romans 5:5).

Our human nature, flesh, is not at all like God's nature, which is Spirit. Only our spirit can join together with His Spirit (see 1 Cor. 6:17). Anything we do with the force of our own willpower is control and borders on witchcraft. When an individual is controlling or "pushy," other people react negatively because it can be felt in the atmosphere. The apostle Paul contrasts the works of the flesh with the fruit of the Spirit and describes the various ways flesh operates:

*Now the works of the flesh are evident, which are: adultery, fornication, uncleanness, lewdness, idolatry, sorcery, hatred, contentions, jealousies, outbursts of wrath, selfish ambitions, dissensions, heresies, envy, murders, drunkenness, revelries, and the like; of which I tell you beforehand, just as I also told you in time past, that those who practice such things will not inherit the kingdom of God* (Galatians 5:19-21).

Anything we do in the flesh opens us up to demonic influence. *Idolatry* arises from lust for a person, place, or thing. *Witchcraft* is the Greek word *pharmakia*, from which we derive our word *pharmacy*. In the King James Version of the Bible, *pharmakia* is translated "witchcraft" because almost no one but witches and sorcerers used drugs during the time the Bible was written. Drug usage was common in pagan worship to induce hallucinations and get in touch with evil spirits.

> *Anything we do in the flesh opens us up to demonic influence.*

We cannot exert our own willpower and be in the Spirit. When we are in the Spirit, we yield to God's will and His life manifests in us and through us. Notice that idolatry and witchcraft are included as "works of the flesh." Anything we do in the flesh opens us up to demonic influence and borders on evil.

*For rebellion is as the sin of witchcraft, and stubbornness is as iniquity and idolatry* (1 Samuel 15:23).

*Rebellion* means to be contentious, refractory, or disobedient toward authority, including God. All rebellion is ultimately against God. *Stubbornness* refers to pressing, pushing, and being insolent. It implies insisting on your own way and using willpower to get it.

*Iniquity* is defined as the working of corrupt desires. It comes from a root word meaning to pant or exert oneself. All three are the product of human willpower.

*All rebellion is against God.*

## Practice: Idolatry and Agendas

To dislodge an idol and give that part of your heart back to God you must first acknowledge its reality. Allow God to reveal an idol by closing your eyes and praying.

**First.** Ask God to show you if you have an idol.

**Feel.** If something (or someone) comes to mind, feel the feeling in the gut. It will feel like titillation, a "pull," or strong desire.

**Forgive.** Receive forgiveness from Christ in you.

**Release.** Release the idol from the gut into the hands of God. Then welcome His presence to fill that area.

## FOUR CHOICES OF THE WILL

In the natural, when faced with pressure our will has three choices, and all three are products of our willpower. We can fight back, run away in fear, or be a doormat and let people "walk all over us." None of those choices are godly responses, however, and we end up feeling stressed or depressed.

When we fight back we fight control with control. If we avoid certain people or situations, we let fear be our guide rather than God. When we quit trying we get angry at ourselves for buckling under, our anger turns inward, and we become depressed. One definition of depression is "anger turned inward." A good question to ask yourself if you begin feeling depressed is, "What do I want that I am not getting?"

When we answer that question, we know what we need to release into the hands of God, who is our genuine source of help.

How then should we live? How can we deal with people and circumstances that feel controlling? No one can control someone who is under God's control. The life of Jesus demonstrates the power of living fully submitted to our heavenly Father.

Believers have a fourth option for the will—to yield our will to the will of Father God! Jesus Himself demonstrated this option. The Gospel of Luke describes an incident in which Jesus read from the book of Isaiah in the synagogue and announced that He was the fulfillment of the prophecy He had just read. The people present were "filled with wrath" and had every intention to throw Jesus over a cliff. Jesus didn't fight them, run from them, or let them shove Him off the hill to His death. He simply walked right through the crowd.

He was only one and they were many. Why didn't they grab hold of Him to stop Him? Because Jesus was under His Father's control, they were unable to touch Him. It was not the will of the Father. When we are yielded to God, we are under His control. No one can control us if we are yielded to the will of the Father. When we are yielded to God, we are at peace and have the inner assurance that God is in complete control of our lives.

> *So all those in the synagogue, when they heard these things, were filled with wrath, and rose up and thrust Him out of the city; and they led Him to the brow of the hill on which their city was built, that they might throw Him down over the cliff. Then passing through the midst of them, He went His way* (Luke 4:28–30).

**No one can control someone
under God's control.**

## ADRENALINE ADDICTION

I (Jen) am a hard worker. I really enjoyed getting A's in school. It gave me a great deal of satisfaction, and I always attempted to get the top score in the class. However, in the kingdom of God we are rewarded for resting, not striving.

When Dennis and I began to do traveling ministry, I enjoyed all the projects and preparation. But I needed to learn that adrenaline was not anointing. Dennis came to me one time while I was rushing around and said, "I feel that we are supposed to be praying right now." I left my busy work and dutifully sat down, but was surprised that I couldn't feel the presence of God immediately.

When I mentioned "my problem" to Dennis, he told me that *I* was the problem. "You need to receive forgiveness for that willpower energy. It opens a door to religious spirits!" I was horrified and received forgiveness immediately. As soon as I did, I felt the presence of God again. That was an important lesson for me to learn! I certainly don't want a rush from willpower to be a substitute for the Holy Spirit in my life!

> *Religious spirits hitchhike*
> *on human willpower.*

Living in stress has become an addiction for many people, even in the ministry. High levels of stress hormones are generally perceived as discomfort and anxiety. However, a person may get used to living in a state of high alert and begin to enjoy the adrenaline "rush" produced.[1] Eventually, the adrenaline addict may even feel they need the energy and "mood boost" to function in everyday life.

Pressure, tension, frustration, anxiety, and a feeling of drivenness are not good. They are *alarms* telling us something is out of kilter and our willpower has kicked in. However, some people rely on a dopamine rush of excitement to counteract an unpleasant feeling of pressure. While that may temporarily relieve the pressure, it can become an addictive loop of "workaholism," competition, extreme sports (such as sky diving), religious hype, pornography, and so forth. But after the high diminishes, frustration or anxiety quickly returns. If the cycle isn't broken, a person can continue this pattern until they burn out or become physically ill. Stress undermines our health because it disrupts nearly every system in our body.

An adrenaline rush or hype can become a substitute for the anointing in ministry. When we minister with an anointing, we feel refreshed afterward. *Adrenaline energy* may feel *similar* to anointing, but it is followed by a "crash" and exhaustion. Many people are reluctant to deal with an adrenaline addiction because they enjoy getting high on willpower.

The antidote for the "buzz" that comes from stress hormones is thankfulness—maintaining an attitude of gratitude. When we are genuinely grateful to God, we tap into supernatural joy, which energizes us by the Spirit. *"In everything give thanks; for this is the will of God in Christ Jesus for you"* (1 Thess. 5:18). And, *"The joy of the Lord is your strength"* (Neh. 8:10b).

> But those who wait on the Lord shall renew their strength;
> they shall mount up with wings like eagles, they shall run and
> not be weary, they shall walk and not faint (Isaiah 40:31).

*Gratitude taps into supernatural joy.*

## RELIGIOUS SPIRITS

Evil spirits, including religious spirits, bring us into bondage. Religious spirits use rituals, laws, and traditions to oppress and drive us (see Gal. 4:3,9). On the other hand, the Holy Spirit gently leads us.

## WILL WORSHIP

The apostle Paul uses an unusual phrase translated "will worship" in the King James Version of the Bible. It refers to any religious activity that comes from the force of human *willpower* instead of the Holy Spirit. Religious activity performed with willpower is "hype." Will worship is the product of human willpower driven by religious spirits. Evil spirits enslave and condemn through religious rituals, vain philosophies, and traditions.

The Greek word *stoicheion* refers to animistic or demonic spirits that ally with religious rituals and traditions.[2] English translations also render this phrase *will worship* as "rudiments of the world," "basic principles of the world," and "elements."

> *Wherefore if ye be dead with Christ from the **rudiments of the world**, why, as though living in the world, are ye subject to ordinances,* (touch not; taste not; handle not; which all are to perish with the using;) *after the commandments and doctrines of men? Which things have indeed a shew of wisdom in **will worship**, and humility, and neglecting of the body; not in any honour to the satisfying of the flesh* (Colossians 2:20-23 KJV).

> *But now after you have known God, or rather are known by God, how is it that you turn again to the weak and beggarly **elements**, to which you desire again to be in bondage?* (Galatians 4:9)

The word *stoicheion* can also be used for Gentile cults and Jewish theories and philosophies called "philosophy and vain deceit."

> *Beware lest any man spoil you through **philosophy and vain deceit**, after the tradition of men, after the rudiments of the world, and not after Christ* (Colossians 2:8 KJV).

When we give in to will worship, or religious rituals and tradition, we come under the influence of religious spirits. Religious spirits hitchhike on the fleshly energy exerted in religious rituals and traditions as well as dead religious works. Remember, religious spirits drive but the Holy Spirit gently leads.

---

### *The Holy Spirit gently leads.*

---

## TRUE WORSHIP

As we have seen, much religious activity and forms of worship are unacceptable to God. Jesus tells us that true worship must be in "spirit and truth."

> *But the hour is coming, and now is, when the true worshipers will worship the Father in spirit and truth; for the Father is seeking such to worship Him. God is Spirit, and those who worship Him must worship in spirit and truth* (John 4:23-24).

The Holy Spirit is the *source* of true worship and our emotions are the *conduits* through which worship flows. Worship that is "spirit and truth" flows from our heart and engages our spirit. It is birthed from a relationship with a Person. "The fuel of worship is the truth of a gracious, sovereign God; the furnace of worship is your spirit and the heat of worship is the vital affections of reverence, fear, adoration, contrition, trust, joy, gratitude, and hope."[3]

## Practice: Self-Deliverance from a Religious Spirit

If you are concerned about whether you have a religious spirit operating in your life:

**Pray.** Close your eyes and pray.

**First.** Picture your Christian life and service to God. If you feel peace and no particular area comes to mind, that's good.

**Feel.** We are to let the peace of God rule in our life. If an aspect of religious activity or your Christianity in general stands out, feel the feeling in your gut. You might feel a particular negative emotion or just a sense of pressure. A feeling of internal pressure or anxiety indicates we have been striving in willpower rather than living by the Spirit.

**Forgive.** When you picture any area (such as teaching Sunday school, witnessing, attending meetings, praying and reading your Bible "enough," doing charitable deeds, and so forth) and feel pressure inside, receive forgiveness until it changes to peace.

We put most religious performance standards on ourselves. If another person is involved, forgive them. If you blame God, release forgiveness toward Him. Jesus says His burden is easy and His yoke is light (see Matt. 11:29-30).

**Release.** If you still feel external pressure after you have peace in your heart, yield to Christ the deliverer in you and welcome Him to rise up within you and push off any religious hitchhiker. Continue to yield to Him until you feel the pressure in the atmosphere lift.

### NOTES

1.  People often confuse an adrenaline rush with a dopamine rush. An adrenaline rush occurs when someone is confronted with fear or stress and their heart starts pounding, they feel like they have uncommon strength, and their energy increases. A dopamine rush is experienced when an individual contemplates some person, place, or thing they lust for and their heart starts racing with excitement.

2.  Footnote for Gal. 4:3, *Spirit-Filled Life ®Bible*, (Nashville, TN: Thomas Nelson Publishers, 1991), 1777.

    Elements [*stoicheion* in Greek] translates a Greek word, which originally referred to the triangle on a sundial for determining time by a shadow-line. From there it came to be applied to *a going in order*, advancing in steps or rows, elementary beginnings, and learning the letters of the alphabet. In NT usage, the word refers to the elementary principles of the OT (Heb. 5:12), the rudiments of both Jewish and Gentile religion (here and Col. 2:8, 20) and the material elements of the universe (2 Pet. 3:10, 12).

    Paul's use of the same word in v. 9 ("the weak and beggarly elements"), along with its usage in Col. 2, lends further insight into "elements." He teaches that spirits of the animistic or demonic dimension (v. 8) find easy allegiance with the rituals and philosophies of human religion and tradition. Hence, the elements of the world are actually evil spirits that use the rituals of the Law (v. 10) to enslave and condemn.

3.  J. Piper, "God seeks people to worship Him in spirit and truth," (Piper's Notes Sermon Library, April 8, 1984). July 25, 2014 http://www.pipersnotes.com/piper84/040884m.htm.

# SECTION THREE

# ADVANCING THE KINGDOM

*Chapter 17*

# THE POWER OF PEACE

When I (Dennis) was a relatively new believer, I had an astounding experience with the power of peace. A local Christian ministry served as a halfway house for convicts, and I volunteered to help out. Those of us who worked there had noticed that every time an inmate was going to make a break for it or do something violent, the atmosphere became charged with negative energy. On one particular day, a sense of danger became so strong the hair stood up on the back of my neck. I knew something really bad must be up.

Suddenly an inmate bolted into the kitchen and grabbed a vicious-looking butcher knife, intending to make a break for it. Because I was standing directly in front of the only exit, he threatened to cut me to pieces me if I didn't move out of the way. However, a powerful peace both filled and surrounded me, so I stood my ground. Although the incident lasted just a few minutes, it seemed like an eternity. Suddenly the man's hand started to tremble and the knife clattered to the floor. Falling to his knees, he began to cry. Supernatural peace really did guard my heart and mind as well as keep me safe physically (see Eph. 6:15).

Ordinarily, I would recommend moving out of the way when confronted with a lethal weapon, but in this case I felt led to stand still.

*The peace of God, which surpasses all understanding, will guard your hearts and minds through Christ Jesus* (Philippians 4:7).

*The God of peace will crush Satan under your feet* (Romans 16:20).

Peace proved to be a militant force in this frightening situation, empowering me to stand while God worked on my behalf. It is not just tranquility or absence of conflict but a mighty force. What is this *peace* that subdues rage and surrounds us with deliverance?

## PEACE IS POWER

Peace is the power that allowed Jesus to pass right through a crowd intending to throw Him over a cliff (see Luke 4:16–30), the creative force of the Living Word at the time of creation (see Gen. 1). Peace is the cohesive force holding the whole universe together (see Col. 1:16-17; Heb. 1:1–3). Peace formed the bonds of one accord that allowed the glory of heaven to be released to earth (see Acts 2:2; 4:31; Eph. 4:3).

Jesus does not fear the storms in people's hearts or the storms of nature. As the Peacemaker, He brought deliverance and peace to the raging Gadarene demoniac (see Mark 5:1–15). The Prince of Peace said, *"Peace, be still"* to a storm and the wind and waves obeyed Him (see Mark 4:39). When we understand the authority of Jesus as the Prince of Peace His words take on a much more profound meaning. The Prince of Peace has given us the gift of *His peace.*

*Peace I leave with you, My peace I give to you; not as the world gives do I give to you. Let not your heart be troubled, neither let it be afraid* (John 14:27).

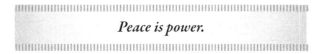

*Peace is power.*

## PEACE IS ABUNDANT LIFE

The Hebrew word for *peace* is *shalom*. The *shalom* of God includes wholeness, peace, health and healing, welfare, safety, salvation, deliverance, soundness, prosperity, perfectness, fullness, rest, harmony, no injustice, and no pain.

Peace is the *essence* of the elusive abundant life promised by Jesus!

> *The thief comes only in order to steal and kill and destroy. I came that they may have and enjoy life, and have it in abundance* (to the full, till it overflows) (John 10:10 AMPC).

*Peace is abundant life!*

The kingdom of God is the triumphant manifestation of supernatural peace that will someday embrace all creation. Jesus was the living expression of the kingdom in His life and ministry on earth. He instructed His disciples to pray for His kingdom to come and His will to be done *"on earth as it is in heaven"* (Matt. 6:10) and sent them forth to proclaim and demonstrate the kingdom. The Holy Spirit empowers us for this same purpose—expanding God's kingdom.

> *Seek first the kingdom of God and His righteousness* (Matthew 6:33a).

When we tap into the power of peace, it's life-changing.

> *Peace is life-changing.*

## ATMOSPHERE CHANGERS

For us to live in kingdom peace, walk in kingdom authority, and operate in kingdom power, Jesus must first conquer our heart: *"Draw near to God and He will draw near to you. Cleanse your hands...and purify your hearts"* (James 4:8). But it doesn't stop there. The apostle Paul prays for us to move far beyond shallow Christianity and *"have the richest measure of the divine Presence"* in our lives, by being *"wholly filled and flooded with God Himself"* (Eph. 3:19 AMPC).

We don't have to be victims of people or circumstances. We should be atmosphere *changers*—militant sons and daughters of the kingdom! All believers have the same spiritual equipment; they only need to be trained to use it. Scripture tells us that Christ gave the five-fold ministers as gifts to the church to equip the saints. Church leaders are not called to be performers but equippers so God's people will be trained.

> *Now these are the gifts Christ gave to the church: the apostles, the prophets, the evangelists, and the pastors and teachers. Their responsibility is to equip God's people to do His work and build up the church, the body of Christ.* (Ephesians 4:11-12 NLT).

While Katy was visiting with several relatives, one of them had an angry meltdown and flipped completely out of control. Katy had been to many of our classes and meetings where we taught about the power of peace. So she decided, "I am going to change this bad atmosphere in here." She did not just stay in peace, she became militant. First, she "dropped down" to Jesus in her heart, and then "blasted" (her word) rivers of peace and love into the atmosphere. Peace flooded the room and the out-of-control relative calmed down.

*Peace blasts into chaos and
calms raging hearts.*

A pastor was in line to make a purchase—the fourth customer from the counter in a convenience store. He had attended classes we'd held in his area. The store clerk was being particularly rude and surly to each person. The pastor thought, "I am going to try what I heard Dennis and Jennifer say in the class." So he let a river of peace and love flow toward the clerk, and by the time it was the pastor's turn the clerk was smiling and pleasant.

*Be filled and flooded with God!*

*Chapter 18*

# THE ADVANCING KINGDOM

Father God has promised Jesus not just the souls of individual believers but a kingdom on earth: *"Ask of Me, and I will give You the nations for Your inheritance, and the ends of the earth for Your possession"* (Ps. 2:8). As representatives of our King, we have been given an assignment to preach and demonstrate kingdom authority *"in demonstration of the Spirit and of power"* (1 Cor. 2:4).

*As the Father has sent Me, I also send you* (John 20:21).

> The authority for deliverance is not just available to a select few in the church. It is available to all believers. Deliverance is the children's bread, a New Testament reality won for us by Jesus on the cross....
>
> Jesus came to set the captives free and commissioned us to continue this work in His name. The advance of His kingdom involves a continuing "jail break" for people who have been imprisoned by the devil. When people are set free from entanglement with the enemy, they are able to come into the fullness of who God intends them to be.[1]

Jesus came as our Deliverer to rescue us and break the chains of bondage that grip mankind. Because of the finished work of the Cross, He has already won the victory. We simply enter into what Jesus has already accomplished on our behalf.

> *For this purpose the Son of God was manifested, that He might destroy the works of the devil* (1 John 3:8b).

## REVELATORY WARFARE

Several years ago, I (Dennis) had a vision of Jesus as a mighty warrior with muscles bulging, sweat on His brow, giving a great shout of victory as He burst through an evil, slimy net of agendas, idolatry, seducing spirits, and demonic soul ties. The snares holding the body of Christ captive were ripped apart and a verse of Scripture was quickened to me: *"The Lord shall go forth like a mighty man; He shall stir up His zeal like a man of war. He shall cry out, yes, shout aloud; He shall prevail against His enemies"* (Isa. 42:13).

Soon after this vision, we received an impartation and activation for what we call "revelatory warfare prayer."[2] While we were praying with our pastoral team for the deliverance of a young mother, we did not receive guidance from the Lord about *what* to pray, God showed us *what He was doing* while we prayed.

As we prayed in the Spirit, we began to see visions of Father God, the Lord Jesus Christ, and the angelic armies of heaven waging war against principalities and powers on our behalf. We saw angels fighting evil beings and God setting up angelic guards to prevent the enemy from returning. Jesus rode forth on a white horse in righteous fury followed by a powerful and vast angelic army.

Every time we saw something, we shared what God was revealing. The fact that we were seeing the same things was confirmation and built up our faith. While we prayed in the Spirit, Father God accomplished the warfare! Later that same day, the young woman for whom we had been praying began to "come into her right mind" and was soon completely restored![3]

A new day is upon us ushering in greater power, gifting, and insight about deliverance. The Lord is releasing revelation so we can have breakthroughs in areas that once seemed difficult...or even impossible. In addition, Jesus is connecting spiritual mothers and fathers who are equipped to disciple the great harvest that is coming (see Eph. 4:3; John 4:35). By delivering, maturing, and bringing us into kingdom alignment, Jesus is preparing *His* net: *"I will build My church, and the gates of Hades shall not prevail against it"* (Matt. 16:18).

> *As we prayed, Father God accomplished the warfare!*

## DELIVERER, FORGIVER, COMFORTER

A friend of ours discovered a profoundly significant truth, but he is a scholar and wasn't really interested in teaching about it. Scholars sometimes get more joy in the discovery process, finding nuggets, than teaching about them. It concerns the double "I AM, I AMs" found exclusively in the Book of Isaiah (see Isa. 43:11,25; 51:12).

The Hebrew word *ani* is used whenever someone talks about themselves, such as, "I went for a walk." Not only can I go for a walk, but anyone else can, too. The distinctive Hebrew word used in Isaiah for "I AM" is *anochi*. What is so significant about this? *Anochi* is used when referring to oneself alone as opposed to everyone else—I and no other. *Anochi* also means the speaker is expressing a desire to get close to the person they are addressing, and it implies intimate relationship between the speaker and the one spoken to.[4]

What should we understand about *anochi* when doubled? The importance of a teaching in the Bible is signified by the use of doubled words. We are thus alerted to the introduction of a weighty matter with profound significance. When God calls Himself as *Anochi Anochi* toward us, He is giving us notice that we have a special and exclusive relationship with Him and it is vital for us to understand.

Therefore, the only way you can fully render the meaning of these three double I AMs is, "I AM, I AM God with an attitude about this!" It's a good attitude, of course, but one of great fervency. In other words, *Anochi, Anochi* as used in the Book of Isaiah means, "I AM, I AM fervent about these things! I AM passionate about delivering, forgiving, and comforting you, and I AM the only One who can do this!"

These three imperative statements in Isaiah are uniquely powerful statements from the heart of Father God toward us (see Isa. 43:11,25; 51:12). They reflect the burning passion of our heavenly Father on our behalf. He desires to deliver, forgive, and comfort us to the uttermost. Deliver us how? Back to the *heart of the Father* who spoke us into existence on planet earth.

We, as children of our heavenly Father, should share His deep desire to rescue those who are in bondage. He wants to express His heart through us. In the mission statement of Jesus, He announced that He had been sent to *"proclaim liberty to the captives"* (Luke 4:18). Now the Lord invites *us* to co-labor with Him on behalf of others. May the fire of His love burn in us!

> *I heard the voice of the Lord, saying: "Whom shall I send, and who will go for Us?" Then I said, "Here am I! Send me"* (Isaiah 6:8).

---

*May the fire of God's love burn in us!*

---

### *We are delivered to be deliverers.*

> *Moreover, we have seen and we testify that the Father has sent his Son as Deliverer of the world* (1 John 4:14 CJB).

> *I, even I, am the Lord, and besides Me there is no savior [deliverer]* (Isaiah 43:11).

> *Then Peter said, "Silver and gold I do not have, but what I do have I give you: In the name of Jesus Christ of Nazareth, rise up and walk"* (Acts 3:6).

> *Paul, greatly annoyed, turned and said to the spirit, "I command you in the name of Jesus Christ to come out of her." And he came out that very hour* (Acts 16:18).

### *We are forgiven to be forgivers.*

> *I, even I, am He who blots out your transgressions [as your forgiver] for My own sake; and I will not remember your sins* (Isaiah 43:25).

### *We are comforted to be comforters.*

> *I, even I, am He who comforts you. Who are you that you should be afraid?* (Isaiah 51:12)

> *Blessed be the God and Father of our Lord Jesus Christ, the Father of mercies and God of all comfort, who comforts us in all our tribulation, that we may be able to comfort those who are in any trouble, with the comfort with which we ourselves are comforted by God* (2 Corinthians 1:3-4).

---

### *We are delivered to be deliverers!*

---

## NOTES

1.  R. Clark, *The Biblical Guide to Deliverance*, (Lake Mary, FL: Charisma House, 2015), 162.

2.  *Revelatory warfare* is a type of corporate intercession. When intercessors come together with hearts knit in true one accord, they pray under a corporate anointing and can then pray God's prayer requests in corporate intercession. Revelatory warfare is warring in our prayer language "from the Holy of Holies." Great power is released in this type of prayer. Although we don't recommend dealing directly with principalities and powers, in revelatory warfare God can and will displace the enemy over the lives of individuals and regions when He gives an assignment to intercede (see Jude 1:1). When we pray the heart of the Father in this way, *He* engages the enemy and accomplishes the warfare on our behalf.

3.  We continued to pray over the next couple of months until a time of temptation had passed and restoration was complete.

4.  Rabbi D. Sperling, *"Ani and Anochi,"* Hebrew Language: Ask the Rabbi, General Questions, Sivan 8, 5773. Yeshiva.org.il, The Torah World Gateway. Retrieved February 18, 2016 from http://www.yeshiva.co/ask/?id=6355.

# ABOUT DENNIS AND DR. JEN CLARK

Dennis and Dr. Jen minister together as a husband and wife team, pastoring Kingdom Life Church in Fort Mill, South Carolina. They are also founder/directors of Full Stature Ministries and TEAM Embassy, an equipping center with an online school at http://training.teamembassy.com. Dr. Jen holds a Th.D. in theology and B.S., M.S. and Ed.S. degrees in psychology.

Printed in Great Britain
by Amazon

41862248R00126